Sis, Break Up with BOAZ

Hope for every frustrated single Christian woman

CYNTHIA HICKERSON

ISBN: 979-8-218-84989-4

Published by: TaylorMade 83 Atlanta, GA.

To my mother, Carlene, my greatest encourager, whose prayers built the foundation under my feet, and whose pride in me will carry me all my days.

To my father, Johnny, whose courage and unwavering faith showed me the heart of God, and whose love for Him lives on through me. Thank you for that gift.

Contents

Introduction

Let's be real. You are probably tired of hearing *"just focus on God"* every time you express that you want to be married. You are tired of the half-smile responses and the Bible verses that are instantly quoted to you that feel like they are meant to quiet your desire instead of help you navigate it. You already know you should focus on God. That is not the problem. The problem is nobody taught you how to honor your desire for marriage while keeping Him first.

This is not a "stop wanting marriage" lecture. It is not a call to bury your desire and pretend you are fine. It is an open conversation that will hopefully bring both clarity and conviction. We will walk through what it looks like to deepen your walk with God, and talk in-depth about dating, attraction, desire, boundaries, and the messy middle between prayer and real life. This is the book you'll wish someone had handed to you years ago when you first started feeling the gap between what you were taught and what you actually experienced. I know I wish I'd had something like this.

I used to think I was waiting on a man.
Not just any man. *My Boaz.*

For years, I believed my life would finally make sense once I got married. I would not feel so overlooked. I would not struggle with sexual temptation. I would not be lonely anymore. And if I'm being real, I thought marriage would somehow make me a spiritual heavyweight — like I would level up in my faith just because I had a ring on my finger.

Somewhere deep down, I saw marriage as the reward for righteousness. I started to believe that the more I strived to be "good," the quicker God would send my husband. So, I told myself I was waiting expectantly, but deep down, I really had a sense of entitlement: like God owed me a *happily ever after* simply because I professed to be a Christian.

And I know I am not the only one who has felt this way.

If you have been in church long enough, you have heard it. *"Just wait for Boaz."* It sounds harmless and even inspiring, but for many of us, those words left more confusion than clarity. We were told to wait. Few of us were taught how. The result was pressure without a clear path. We were given a love story in Ruth as a how-to guide for marriage, but with very little direction on how to live whole, God-filled lives in the meantime.

Wanting marriage is a God-given desire. It is natural. It is beautiful. And it is nothing to be ashamed of.

But here is where it gets tricky. Without realizing it, we can take a good thing and quietly give it more weight than it was ever meant to carry.

That is what I did. The closer I got to what I thought was the promise, the more my unhealed wounds started to surface: abandonment issues, a need to control, insecurity, and a loud hunger to be loved. I thought I was walking toward a blessing, but I was slowly building my identity around it.

And that identity unraveled when my marriage ended in divorce. What I discovered in the aftermath was not just heartbreak. It was the realization that I had built my worth on something that could be taken away. I also realized that my desire was shaped more by my flesh than my faith, and my "why" was rooted in selfish desires, not spiritual ones.

And if any of that sounds familiar, you're not alone.

That's what *"Break Up with Boaz"* really means. It's the moment you stop waiting for a man to validate what Jesus already settled. It's about checking the "why" of your heart and remembering that marriage is a desire, not a demand. And it's about releasing the quiet frustration with God that builds after every heartbreak, when you can't understand why He allows it. Breaking up with Boaz isn't a rejection of love; it's a release. It's surrender. It's saying, "Lord, You can have this desire, too."

And when I call you "Sis" I'm not just using a nickname. I'm speaking to you as my *Sister in Christ*. This isn't internet slang. It's family language. It's how I remind both of us that this conversation is happening between daughters of God: women who are learning, healing, and walking toward wholeness together.

Sis, this book is my open letter to you: the you who has prayed, hoped, maybe even cried for marriage, and still wonders why the wait still feels like a weight. I am not here to tell you to stop desiring it. I am here to help you break up with mindsets that keep you from living free in the meantime.

The truth is you do not have to wait for Boaz for your purpose to be complete. You do not need a ring to know you are chosen. You are not on spiritual probation because you are single.

I wrote this because I wish someone had told me sooner that God's best for me was never a man. It was always Himself. I wish I would've learned sooner that His love, His voice, and His presence are not a consolation prize for when marriage takes too long. They are the very thing that makes life rich now.

So, if you are tired of timelines, tired of pressure, and tired of wondering when it is your turn, this is your invitation to let God take marriage off the pedestal and put it back in its rightful place as a blessing, not a burden.

1 | My Obsession with Boaz

Some of us have prayed for a husband. Some of us have prepared for him like he is already on the way. And some of us, if we are being honest, have been so focused on the idea of Boaz that we forgot to nurture our relationship with the God who writes the story. I know, because that was me.

When I was thirty-one, the dating pool felt more like a puddle. I had just ended things with a man who, on paper, looked like everything I wanted. He was kind. He showed up. He said the right things. But something felt off. I could feel deep down that this effort came from an obligation to portray himself as a "good guy" and not a genuine desire to pursue *me*. I felt like I was a checklist item. A project. I was tired of being someone's performance review. I walked away.

The break-up was necessary, but it left me drained. Not in a crying-on-the-floor way, but in a "What is even the point of dating anymore?" way. I started to believe that the *nice, Christian guy routine* was just another role some men played until they got bored, with no real desire to pursue, commit, or build.

Out of frustration, I took my bruised heart to God and said, *"If You want me to be married, You do it. I quit."* I didn't know it then, but those words were a turning point. I was finally taking the first steps to surrendering my love life, the one area that I had subconsciously refused to let God touch before.

I began spending more intentional time in the Word. Praying. Worshiping. Talking to Him about everything. That's also when I began praying for my future husband. I would write him letters, journal about our life together, and imagine what it would be like to share love, ministry, and purpose.

At first, it felt holy. It felt like hope. But slowly, my focus shifted. I was daydreaming more about a man I had never met than about the God who was here now. Somewhere, hope had turned into habit. I'd walk into church and scan the room, wondering if he was there. I wasn't just going to hear the Word. I was secretly hoping to be seen. I told myself I was "just preparing" for marriage.

Have you ever caught yourself hoping to be seen more than you came to see God?

Maybe you have never done that, and your story looks nothing like mine. But for me, my desire for marriage became the loudest voice in my life. Somewhere along the way, waiting stopped feeling like preparation and started feeling like punishment. And judging by the stories I've heard from other women, I know I'm not alone.

The Problem With the "Boaz Blueprint"

If you have been in church long enough, you have probably heard it: *"Just wait for your Boaz."* It is often said with love and good intentions, but over time it has become less of a biblical encouragement and more of a catchy slogan that gets passed around like a Christian fairy tale.

The truth is, Boaz has been commercialized. Over the years, he has been turned into the Christian version of Prince Charming: the wealthy, Godly man who notices you in a crowd, rescues you, and carries you off to a life of love and security. It sounds romantic, but that version of Boaz does not exist in the Bible.

If you want to read the full story for yourself, you can find it in the book of Ruth. And when you read it closely, you will notice some important details that are often left out when this story is used as dating advice.

The first thing is this: the reason Boaz married Ruth was not because they had some instant, deep, spiritual connection or because he was so in love with her. Boaz married Ruth because it was the customary, lawful thing to do as her kinsman-redeemer. That fancy title meant he had the right to marry her to preserve her late husband's family line. In fact, Boaz was not even the first in line. There was another relative who had the right to marry Ruth before him, and Boaz met with this man to see if he wanted to take on that role. When the other man declined, Boaz stepped in. This was a legal transaction rooted in Israelite law, not whirlwind romance.

The second thing is this: Ruth did not just sit back and wait for Boaz to pursue her. In fact, the Bible tells us that Naomi, her mother-in-law, came up with a plan for Ruth to approach Boaz. She instructed Ruth to wash, put on her best clothes, and go to the place where Boaz would be. Ruth followed Naomi's plan and made her intentions known. In other words, Ruth's story is not a passive "be found" moment. It was a strategic, intentional move based on Naomi's wisdom.

When these pieces get left out, we are left with a one-dimensional, idealized picture of Boaz that is not accurate. And if we build a "marriage blueprint" from a romanticized version of this story, we end up with expectations that the Bible never promised. Now, does that mean Ruth and Boaz's story has nothing to teach us? Absolutely not. But the lessons are not about sitting still until someone notices you.

Here is what the Bible actually shows us.

The story is about Ruth's faithfulness to God in a place that was unfamiliar. It is about her covenant with Naomi, a relationship rooted in loyalty and sacrifice. It is about Boaz's integrity as a man of God who acted with honor toward a vulnerable woman.

Ruth was not passively waiting. She was working with integrity, following wise counsel, and moving in alignment with God's plan. Boaz was not simply "looking for a wife." He was living out his purpose and letting his character speak for him.

The Overlooked Part of Ruth's Story

When we ignore those truths and turn Ruth's story into a fairy tale template, we strip away its depth and set ourselves up for shallow expectations that do not prepare us for real life.

One of the most powerful parts of Ruth's story is her loyalty to Naomi. Ruth 1:16 is not just a poetic line. It is a covenant.

"Don't ask me to leave you and turn back. Wherever you go, I will go; wherever you live, I will live. Your people will be my people, and your God will be my God" (Ruth 1:16 NLT).

Ruth first committed herself to God, a God she had only come to know through her relationship with Naomi. She had seen His hand on Naomi's life, even in loss, and chose to follow Him because of the witness Naomi had been.

That covenant friendship positioned her for everything that followed. Ruth's relationship with Naomi was built on trust, mutual respect, and a shared commitment to God. That was not just a background detail. It was a key part of how God moved in her life.

We will go deeper into the importance of these kinds of friendships in Chapter 6, but for now remember this. Ruth's life was already full of Godly relationships before she ever met Boaz.

When we turn Boaz into the whole point of the story, we miss the richness of what God was doing before the romance even began. We forget that the foundation for a Godly marriage is built long before you ever meet the man.

The Shift That Changed Everything

I am not asking you to stop wanting marriage or throw away the story of Ruth and Boaz. I am inviting you to see both through a different lens.

For me, breaking up with my obsession with Boaz was not about giving up on love. It was about replacing my view of marriage as the ultimate life achievement with the Biblical truth that marriage is a calling before it ever is a commitment.

Marriage is a good thing. A holy thing. A gift from God. But even good things can be dangerous when they hold more weight in our hearts than God Himself. That is what makes marriage idolatry so tricky. It hides under the language of faith. It sounds like surrender: "I am just waiting on God's timing" or "I am just waiting on my Boaz." Yet for me, there was a deeper truth I had to face.

I did not recognize it at first, because it did not look like rebellion. It looked like hope. It looked like vision boards and faith confessions. But that desire began to dictate my joy, my peace, and even my relationship with God, and I realized I was no longer worshiping Him. I was worshiping a dream.

Just like the Israelites, I had created a golden calf.
But mine was a wedding ring.

That was my story. Yours may look completely different. But if you have ever felt your desire for marriage weighing heavy on your heart, shaping the way you see yourself, or quietly influencing your relationship with God, I want to invite you into an honest reflection.

Could it be that marriage has taken a place in your life it was never meant to hold?

For me, it took time to admit it. I started treating marriage like proof that I was worthy, whole, and chosen. I believed the wait was punishment for my past or evidence that something was wrong with me. That belief grew louder every time someone asked why I was still single or when I was going to have children. As the years passed, those questions carried more weight. Society whispers, "If you were really complete, you would not still be alone." And slowly, I started to believe it.

That mindset left me drained. I dated for the wrong reasons—validation. For distraction. For escape. I performed and tried to earn a relationship like it was a spiritual reward. In the end, I burned myself out chasing an idol I had unknowingly built.

So, let's be honest, Sis. We can love God and still place something else above Him in our hearts. We can serve faithfully and still be motivated by fear instead of faith. We can want marriage and still need God to lift the weight we have put on it.

Before We Talk About Marriage...

Here's the thing. The weight didn't just show up one day. Most of us learned how to carry it. We were handed it in sermons, Bible studies, women's conferences, and well-meaning advice. That's why before we talk about marriage itself, we need to talk about where our ideas about it were born. For many of us, they started in church.

...

Reflection

Before we move forward, take a moment to be honest with yourself and God. These questions are not here to shame you or make you second-guess your desires. They are here to help you see your heart clearly so you can carry it to the next chapter with an open mind and an open spirit.

1. *Has marriage quietly become the goal of your faith journey?*
2. *What emotions surface when you imagine never getting married?*
3. *In what ways has your desire for marriage affected your closeness with God?*

2| The Church Said Wait

One of the loudest voices in shaping how many of us see marriage has been the Church. A lot of what we've been taught is beautiful and rooted in truth. Some of it is...not. And that can be hard to talk about when you love the Church. My faith was nurtured in church pews, prayer meetings, and worship nights, which is why it matters to me that we talk honestly about some of the messages we've received about marriage. This isn't about throwing shade at the Church. It is about making sure that what we've learned lines up with God's truth.

Found Doesn't Mean Invisible

One of the most repeated marriage verses in church circles is Proverbs 18:22. *"He who finds a wife finds a good thing, and obtains favor from the Lord"* (Proverbs 18:22 NKJV). I have heard it quoted in sermons, Bible studies, and women's conferences more times than I can count. And almost every time, it comes with the same message for single women: *"Wait to be found."*

Sounds harmless, right? But here is the problem: that is not exactly what this verse says. In the original Hebrew, the word *matsa,* (which translates to *find* in English) means "to discover, to attain, to acquire, to encounter" (Strong's H4672). It implies movement and intention — it's not a man stumbling across you but a man encountering you as he moves in purpose. And when he encounters you, he realizes that who you are and what you carry inside you is needed to help him carry out his God-given assignment.

One of the clearest signs a woman is ready to be a wife is not that she has perfected domestic skills or fits someone's Instagram version of "wifey." It is that she is a woman full of wisdom — the kind that only comes from walking closely with God and obeying His voice. That kind of woman doesn't just get "found." She gets identified. Not just as a wife, but as *his* wife.

Yet, somewhere along the way, the truth about what it means to be "found" got watered down. Instead of being taught how to live in wisdom and purpose, many of us were told to shrink ourselves and wait in the background until a man appeared. But Proverbs 18:22 was never about a woman hiding and hoping. It is about both people walking in alignment with God's plan until their paths cross. That is the kind of "waiting" God calls us to: not idleness, but purposeful living.

Active vs. Passive Waiting

When I talk about "waiting," I am not saying your life has to be on hold until a man arrives. Many women are already living fully, building careers, deepening their walk with God, and enjoying rich friendships. If that is you, then you already know the kind of fulfillment that comes from walking in purpose before marriage.

But for others, "waiting" has been taught as standing still. That version of waiting will leave you restless and unprepared. The kind of waiting God invites us into is active trust. It is living in motion while keeping your heart in step with His timing.

The Proverbs 31 woman is often quoted like a hashtag. *"I'm a Proverbs 31 woman"* sounds cute on a mug or a T-shirt. But when you read Proverbs 31:10-31, you find a woman who is far from idle. She buys fields, plants vineyards, runs her household, serves her community, and honors God through her work. And here is something worth thinking about. Although this passage describes her as a wife, she did not suddenly become this woman after marriage. It is safe to say she was already living in wisdom, diligence, and purpose long before she had the title. That is likely how she was identified as a wife in the first place. Her value was not in waiting to be chosen but in living fully in the role God had already given her.

That kind of life positions you for Godly marriage if it is a part of your story, but it is also fulfilling and fruitful whether marriage comes or not. Active waiting means you are already living in such a way that your presence adds value wherever God places you.

Why Passive Waiting Hurts Us

It's interesting how passivity seems to be preached almost exclusively when it comes to dating. In every other area of life, we are told to take intentional steps. If you need a job, you don't just sit by the phone and hope a recruiter calls you out of nowhere. You update your resume, apply for positions, and network. If you want to grow in your career, you take classes, seek mentorship, and look for opportunities to advance.

Yet when it comes to relationships, many women have been told to stay out of sight and a man will one day just show up. That mindset does more than keep you stuck: it can quietly make your faith stagnant. We start to believe that God is going to do all the heavy lifting while we sit back and wait for Him to hand us the desires of our heart. That kind of thinking is dangerous because it teaches us to treat God like a genie instead of our Creator.

It also ignores the reality of free will. God will not override human choice to force someone into your life. When we settle for being passive, we act as if our free will does not exist. We remove ourselves as active participants in the outcome and convince ourselves that "waiting on God" means we bear no responsibility. And if nothing happens — or things do not happen the way we imagined — it becomes easy to blame God for our disappointment. We mean well when we sit still, but faith without motion eventually turns stale. And it keeps us from even exploring the opportunities God may place in front of us. Purposeful positioning is not desperation. It is wisdom. It is the same principle you already live out in your work, your education, your ministry, and your personal growth. The difference is that in dating, wisdom means you keep moving in your God-given purpose, fully visible in the life He has called you to, rather than hiding in the background and calling it "faith."

When the Church Got It Right

Seeing what's been mishandled is only part of the story. There's also beauty in what the Church has taught well, and that deserves space too.

The answer to harmful passivity is not swinging to the other extreme and chasing after relationships in our own strength. Wisdom calls us to find the middle ground: living with intention, while trusting God to align the right connections at the right time. And to be fair, not everything the Church has taught us about marriage is wrong. Most of it is deeply rooted in biblical truth and is important to hold on to. The key is learning to separate the weight of man-made expectations from the freedom of God's design.

One thing the Church gets right is the call to trust God's timing. That is not an excuse to hide, but it is a safeguard against trying to manufacture something God has not ordained. God is not bound by our clocks or calendars. His timing is not defined by human terms, and what is "late" or "too soon" in our eyes is always on time in His. Trusting His timing looks different for every person. It is essential to stay in close communication with Him and walk in obedience so you will know what season you are in.

Another biblical truth the Church upholds is the call to wait until marriage for sexual intimacy. No matter what our culture says, God's design for sex has not changed. Waiting is not about shame or restriction; it is about honoring God's covenant, protecting your heart and your body, and building a foundation that is not clouded by physical compromise. We will talk more about sex later in this book, but it is worth naming here because it is one of the most consistent truths the Church has taught well.

The Church also views marriage as a gift, and that is a good thing. In many congregations, marriage is celebrated as a sacred covenant, not just a social event. The Church has consistently reminded us that marriage is designed to reflect Christ's love for the Church (Ephesians 5:25-32), and that it is meant to be a partnership built on love, service, and mutual respect. In healthy spaces, this high view of marriage inspires couples to honor their vows and gives singles a vision for covenant that is worth pursuing.

The caution is that sometimes the enthusiasm for marriage can overshadow the preparation it requires. The pressure to "just get married" can lead people into covenant without a clear understanding of God's design, without emotional maturity, and without the skills to build a lasting relationship. The goal should be to keep marriage in its rightful place, a beautiful gift within God's bigger purpose, while also preparing people to walk it out well.

Discernment is another truth worth keeping. God's Word warns us not to be unequally yoked (2 Corinthians 6:14), and that principle is not just talking about unbelievers. Not every man who calls himself a Christian is living in obedience to Christ. Guarding your heart and evaluating a man's fruit is a wisdom you cannot afford to throw away.

And here is where the gap still remains. While the Church teaches the importance of marriage and warns against unhealthy relationships, there is often very little practical teaching on *how* to date in a way that honors God. We will dig into that later in *Dating with Discernment*, but for now it is enough to recognize that truth without guidance can still leave you confused and unprepared.

When we hold onto the truths God established, release the traditions that keep us stuck, and fill the gaps with practical wisdom paired with Godly insight, we can honor the parts of the Church's teachings that protect us while also walking in the freedom Christ died to give us.

When Protection Turns Into a Wall

The truth is, most of what we've heard in church about marriage has come from a place of wanting to protect us. The intentions are often good. The challenge is that sometimes protective walls become barriers, especially when it comes to how men and women interact before marriage. In an effort to guard us against sin, we have sometimes built rules that keep us from learning how to have healthy, Godly friendships with the opposite sex. And if we cannot build trust and respect in friendship, how will we ever recognize a partner worth building a life with?

...

Reflection

Before we move into the next chapter, it is worth taking an honest look at how much of what you believe about marriage came from God and how much came from people. Use these questions to check in with yourself and invite Him into the process.

1. *What messages about marriage from the Church have shaped your thinking the most, and do they align with God's Word?*

2. *How do you personally define "active waiting," and what does that look like in your current season of life?*

3. *Which truths from the Church's teaching do you want to hold on to, and where do you see gaps that you need to fill with God's wisdom?*

3| Don't Sit Too Close

There is an unspoken rule in many church circles: keep your distance from the opposite sex unless you are on the road to marriage. We might not announce it from the pulpit, but it shows up in the side-eyes, the whispered comments, and the awkward shuffle people make when a single man and woman sit too close together. The goal is usually "avoid temptation," but the result is that we miss out on building healthy, Godly friendships with men. When friendship is off the table, the only space left for interaction is romance, which puts pressure on relationships before they have a chance to grow.

Where This Rule Comes From

If you grew up in church, you already know that purity is a constant theme. Scripture warns us to flee from sexual immorality, and that is not up for debate. The problem isn't the biblical command; it is how the command has been applied. Over time, fear-based rules began to replace balanced wisdom. Instead of teaching men and women how to interact in a way that honors God, a lot of us were taught to avoid each other altogether.

This overcorrection often comes from a desire to protect people, especially young singles, from sin. The intention may be good, but the outcome is not. Avoidance does not teach maturity. It does not show us how to treat the opposite sex as brothers and sisters in Christ. Instead, it creates an environment where we are either separate or suddenly expected to be marriage material the moment we connect. That is not how healthy relationships are built, and it is not how the body of Christ is meant to function.

The Problem with Overprotection

When the unspoken rule is "keep your distance," it sends a clear message: men and women cannot be in the same space without it meaning something. You either get labeled as "interested" or treated like you might be a temptation. There is no middle ground. No safe space to just be friends.

Here's the problem with that. If the only time we talk to men is when dating is already in the air, we miss out on learning the basics — like how to communicate, how to resolve conflict, and how to just enjoy each other's company without a hidden agenda. Friendships are where you see someone's real character. Without that, dating becomes a gamble with your heart at stake.

If you've ever avoided a conversation with a man at church because you didn't want people whispering, you know what I'm talking about. I've been there. Guarding my every move. Wondering if sitting too close or laughing too hard would be misread. That kind of pressure doesn't just make friendships awkward. It makes dating harder, because we never get the chance to build trust before romance enters the picture.

Have you ever felt like you had to downplay a friendship to look "spiritual enough"?

How This Affected My Relationships

As boys and girls grow up together, it's normal to start developing feelings you don't fully understand. In my experience growing up in church, any visible friendship between a boy and a girl was immediately met with suspicion. If an adult saw us talking or playing, it wasn't seen as innocent — it was treated as inappropriate. The whispers, the warnings, the raised eyebrows. It was if simply being seen with a boy could give you a reputation.

Looking back, I understand the intention to protect us from the dangers of premature relationships. But they missed the mark in one critical way: they never explained that liking someone, developing feelings, or even noticing the opposite sex is a normal part of growing up. They didn't teach us how to steward those feelings or manage our thoughts. They just told us to stay away.

It wasn't a proactive approach. It was a scare tactic. And for me, it backfired. When something is forbidden, it often becomes more enticing. I began to see boys not as people to respect or befriend, but as objects of desire. Crushes turned into fixations. Boys became "the goal," not having brothers in Christ. And since I was never taught how to be friends with a guy, I never learned how to trust them either.

It planted confusion about connection that didn't go away when I grew up. That carried over into my adult life. I went from having little to no platonic interaction with men to suddenly being in dating situations where everything felt intense right away. There was no friendship to ease into. No safe space to build trust first. And because I didn't have that foundation, I struggled to communicate, set healthy boundaries, and see men as whole people rather than potential boyfriends or husbands.

God's View on Platonic Friendships

Here's the truth. The Bible does not give us a long list of detailed examples of platonic friendships between men and women. In biblical times, cultural norms made those kinds of relationships uncommon, so it is harder to find specific examples to point to. That is part of why this topic is often avoided or misunderstood in the Church today.

What we do see in Scripture are plenty of examples of what Godly friendships look like in general, whether it is between two men, two women, or within families. Those principles still apply to relationships with the opposite sex. We will explore some of those examples in depth in the chapter *Brothers Before Boaz*, but for now, it is important to note that men and women did interact in the Bible, even if it wasn't the cultural norm.

And while examples of male-female friendships are rare, we still see glimpses of how God honors mutual respect and spiritual connection. Jesus Himself spoke with women in public, which was surprising in His time. For example, His conversation with the Samaritan woman at the well (John 4:7-26) crossed cultural barriers of gender, ethnicity, and morality. He also welcomed Mary to sit at His feet as a disciple while Martha worked (Luke 10:38-42), showing that women were invited into spiritual depth alongside men.

Scripture also gives us wisdom about friendship in general. *"A friend loves at all times, and a brother is born for a time of adversity"* (Proverbs 17:17 NIV). While that verse does not single out male-female friendship, it shows us that real friendship is built on love, loyalty, and being there for one another in hard times.

Platonic friendships with the opposite sex can sharpen your discernment, teach you respect, and give you a safe environment to understand the mindset of a man without the pressure of trying to be his partner. You're not trying to "figure him out" to win his affection. You are learning how men think, communicate, and approach life, which can help you relate in a healthier way when romance does enter the picture.

Before we talk about dating, we must reclaim what friendship really means.

Why Friendship Matters

Some of the strongest marriages you will ever see started with friendship. Not flirtation. Not constant texting. Not jumping into "What are we?" talks on the second interaction. Just friendship.

Friendship gives you the space to see someone's real character without the pressure of romance clouding your judgment. You notice how they treat people. You see how they handle conflict, stress, or disappointment. You watch how they serve others, how they talk about people when they are not in the room, and how they respond to correction. These are things you cannot always spot when the excitement of a new relationship is pulling your focus.

Building that kind of connection also gives you the gift of time. It allows trust to grow naturally, not because you are rushing toward a commitment, but because you are learning each other in real life. Friendship can reveal deal breakers before you have invested your heart, and it can also confirm alignment in values and purpose without forcing anything.

And here's the reality. If you marry someone you are not friends with, life will feel a lot longer and a lot harder than it has to. Friendship is the foundation you will lean on when attraction fades for a season or life gets messy. Without it, the relationship can feel shallow or fragile when things get tough.

And that's not just theory. I lived it. I learned some of these lessons the hard way. More than once, I let potential friendships turn into awkward almost-relationships because I didn't know how to just be friends with a man. We will talk more about that in *Brothers Before Boaz*, and I will share a story that started the shift of how I see male-female friendships today.

But before we go there, we need to start with who you are in God.

The Relationship That Comes First

Friendship matters. Not just because it can prepare you for a healthy marriage, but because it teaches you how to love people the way God intended: with patience, honor, and a pure heart. And when you know how to give and receive that kind of love, you stop viewing marriage as the only relationship worth investing in.

But here is the deeper truth: God calls us to more than titles. The word "Christian" gets thrown around like a badge of honor, but wearing a title is not the same as living the life. God did not call us to be professional churchgoers. He called us to be disciples. Daughters. People who are willing to lean in, do the heart work, and follow Him.

Because if you don't know who you are to God, you will spend your life trying to find that worth in someone else. That's a spiritual identity crisis. Before anything else, we should talk about what it means to be a daughter before you are ever a bride.

...

Reflection

Before we move forward, take a moment to look back at your own experiences. These questions are not about guilt or regret. They are about clarity. The more honest you are with yourself here, the more prepared you will be for the next chapter.

1. *Have you avoided building friendships with the opposite sex because of fear, assumptions, or church culture?*
2. *How have your views on friendship shaped the way you approach dating and relationships?*
3. *What would it look like for you to start valuing friendship as much as romance?*

4 |Daughters Before Brides

Before I ever understood what it meant to be a wife, I had to face the fact that I barely understood what it meant to be a daughter—not to my biological father, and not to God. I knew the worship songs and how to address God as my heavenly "Father" when I began a prayer. But deep down, I had no idea how to live like I was loved, protected, and chosen by Him. I didn't know how to rest in the safety of being a daughter, because I had never experienced it in my natural life.

So, I did what I thought would earn His approval. I worked hard to be the "good Christian woman" I thought He wanted, hoping it would qualify me for the blessing of marriage. What I didn't realize was that God wasn't asking me to perform for a title. He was inviting me to rest in an identity.

The Mirror Moment

For me, my lack of identity as God's daughter didn't fully hit me until I was three and a half years into a marriage that had started to quietly crumble not long after our first anniversary. Our communication had broken down and so had our trust. We weren't building together anymore; we were just coexisting. Somewhere along the way, we stopped letting God lead us and started making decisions based on emotion. Deep down, I had tied my sense of worth to keeping the marriage together, even when it felt empty. But even worse than that, I didn't like *myself* anymore. I had become unrecognizable.

One day I stood in front of the mirror, eyes red and swollen from another round of tears, my spirit drained. And then I heard a quiet voice, almost like a whisper:

Who are you?

And the truth was...I didn't know.

I was lost. Lost in a relationship that I believed would define me. Lost in the grief of what I thought my life would be. Lost in the disappointment of a reality that didn't match the picture I had in my head.

As the tears kept streaming down my face, I realized they weren't just cries of frustration and desperation, but prayers in disguise. A verse came to mind; one I had read before but had never hit home until that moment:

"You keep track of all my sorrows. You have collected all my tears in your bottle. You have recorded each one in your book." (Psalm 56:8 NLT)

And in that moment, I realized just how intentional God really is. The thought that the Creator of the universe had been paying that much attention to me was almost too much to process. He was not just watching over me but collecting my tears and recording them. Not one moment of my pain had gone unnoticed.

That kind of love...stunned me. And it made me ask, *Why does He think I'm that important?*

It was in that sacred space, face stained with tears and heart wide open, that God started peeling back the layers I had wrapped myself in. He began to show me how much I had clung to the title of "wife" like it was the highest honor I could have. But the title I had ignored was the one that mattered most. I didn't realize it yet, but being His daughter was the highest honor of all.

Have you ever tried to earn a title God already gave you?

How I Erased the Word 'Father'

That moment in front of the mirror was only the beginning. I didn't realize it then, but God was about to uncover the deepest wound of my life: my father wound.

The truth is that the father-daughter dynamic was foreign to me. I was raised by a single mother, not because my father didn't want to be around, but because he couldn't be. He was incapable. Incapacitated mentally, emotionally, and spiritually. Alcohol was his vice.

Some of my earliest memories of him are not warm or safe. They are filled with yelling, staggering, slurred cussing, and the bitter stain of a liquor-soaked kiss on my cheek during one of his rare visits. Even as a little girl, I knew something wasn't right. His behavior scared me. It embarrassed me. And I wanted no part of him.

Eventually, I asked my mom if I could stop seeing him. She respected my request. But my father didn't understand the concept of distance, especially from his only daughter. He would still show up: ringing the apartment doorbell over and over, slurring my name outside. When he realized he wouldn't be let in, he'd put on a show. Yelling. Cussing. Drawing a crowd.

I remember the neighborhood kids laughing and pointing, even throwing rocks. I'd peek out the window, cringing with a mix of disgust and shame, secretly wishing I could pretend he wasn't mine. I wanted a father I could be proud of. Someone kind. Someone safe. Someone present.

Instead, I taught myself to stop expecting anything at all. Slowly, I erased the idea of what a father should be. I convinced myself that I didn't need one. But erasing that idea didn't erase the need.

Daddy Issues

Like me, some of you carry wounds from a father who was absent, addicted, or emotionally unavailable. Maybe you've already named it. Maybe you're still trying to face it.

Others of you grew up with a father who was present, loving, and strong. He was your hero. The kind of man other people admired. But here's the thing: even good dads can become idols. If he was always the one who rescued you, provided for you, and showed up every time, you may have never learned what it means to need God as Father. Where would He fit if your earthly dad seemed to meet every need?

And then there are some of us who fall somewhere in between. Not fully broken, not fully healed.

Wherever your story lands, your earthly father has shaped how you see our heavenly one. To be clear, it's not just a connection— it's a lens. Whether that lens is cracked or crystal clear, it affects the way you trust God, hear from Him, and even how you believe He feels about you.

Identity Crisis

When I decided I didn't need a father, I meant it. In some ways, it even felt true. I had survived without one. I grew up, graduated college as the first in my family, held down jobs, and made my own decisions. I had watched my mother hustle on her own, refuse to give up, and figure things out without waiting for anyone to rescue her: and I learned to do the same. I told myself that kind of determination was all I needed. I learned to navigate life in a world where a father was never required to show up. So, I told myself I was fine.

But survival doesn't mean wholeness. My belief wasn't a complete lie, but it was deeply deceptive. I didn't realize how much it shaped me until years later. As a way to cope, I became whoever I needed to be to feel accepted.

The high-achieving version of me made my mother proud. The agreeable, non-confrontational version made my friends comfortable. The "good girl" image made my elders and church family happy.

And the secret version of me—the one who mastered sexual allure while wearing innocent eyes—was born from a perfect storm of longing for my father, curiosity about boys, and the "don't sit too close" culture I was raised in. My mother, terrified I'd end up pregnant as a teenager, watched me like a hawk before I was even thinking about sex. The constant tension only made boys feel more mysterious and more magnetic.

Longing for Love

But none of those identities were really me. And yet, I carried them into everything: adulthood, dating, marriage, and even my relationship with God.

The achiever in me treated relationships like something I could earn with good behavior and performance.

The agreeable version of me stayed silent when I was hurting because I thought love meant keeping the peace.

The "good girl" in me assumed God would keep extending grace, even when I knew I was living a double life.

And the one who craved male attention? I brought her with me, too. I still wanted to be desired. I still needed someone to make me feel beautiful, chosen, and worthy.

What I didn't realize was that each version of me was still that same little girl longing for the kind of love only a Father could give.

The Missing Title

I used to think I had a "man" problem. But what I really had was a missing title.

Not *wife.*

Not *girlfriend.*

Not *somebody's future.*

The title I was missing was *daughter.*

For most of my life, I had performed for love, adjusted for approval, and hustled for belonging; without realizing I already had it. And until I confronted that truth, every other identity I tried to wear was just a placeholder.

I don't know what your story with your earthly Father looks like. Maybe he was present. Maybe he wasn't. Maybe you've already worked through the pain of that relationship, or maybe you've avoided it altogether. Wherever you are in your journey, I want to invite you to pause and reflect: How has your view of your earthly father, good or bad, shaped the way you see God? The way you trust Him? The way you believe He sees you?

Because the way we see God as Father affects everything. Coming to terms with that truth prepared my heart for what Jesus had been teaching all along.

Why Jesus Taught Us to Pray 'Our Father'

When the disciples asked Jesus to teach them how to pray, He began with two words that changed everything: "Our Father" (Matthew 6:9). This was radical for their day. The Jewish people were used to addressing God by His titles:

Lord, Almighty, Creator. But calling Him *Father* was personal, intimate, and even controversial.

In the language of the Bible, to be called "Son of God" meant to be of the same nature as God. Jesus wasn't simply a man with a special title; He was God in the flesh. So when he told His disciples to address God as Father, He was inviting them into the same kind of relationship He had: one that went beyond a servant-master dynamic into the closeness of family.

This wasn't just about picturing God as a comforting father figure. Knowing Him as Father means recognizing Him as the Triune God — Yahweh — who is not only Creator but also Savior, Deliverer, Healer, and the One who conquered the grave through His resurrection. It means understanding that the God who spoke the world into existence also leans in close enough to hear you when you pray.

That's why it's worth asking: if Jesus wanted us to know God in this way, why wouldn't we want to embrace it fully?

When I Accepted God as Father

For me, this revelation became real over time. As I surrendered more of my life to God, He began to work on my heart toward my natural father. Forgiveness came first in my heart before it ever came out of my mouth. It took years, but eventually, my father and I began to build a relationship. He surrendered his addiction to the Lord, and has been sober for several years. Now we speak weekly, after not speaking for most of my life. And that's nothing short of a testimony to the healing power of God!

But we didn't get here until I realized I needed more than a natural father. I needed a heavenly one.

The truth didn't hit me all at once. It came crashing in when my mother — my constant, my anchor, my only version of family, passed away from breast cancer in 2023. The grief was overwhelming, a kind of pain that is indescribable. I remember thinking, *I'm an orphan now. I don't have anyone.* My father was in my life at that point, but we were still getting to know each other. Our connection felt more like a friendship than a father-daughter bond, and in that moment of grief, it didn't soothe the ache I was feeling.

And in the middle of my lowest moments, God whispered, *I am your Father.* He didn't just say it once. He repeated it, again and again, until it started to sink in. And it wasn't only through an audible whisper. He said it through strangers who showed up for me unexpectedly. He said it in dreams that revealed His plans for me. He said it in conversations where family and friends unknowingly repeated things I had prayed for in secret.

Through all of it, He began teaching me what fatherhood meant: not just as theology, but as reality. In my loneliness, He became my Comforter. In my confusion, He became my Guide. And in my grief, He became the steady, unshakable presence I could lean on.

To Know Him is to Love Him

Knowing God as Father is not just about memorizing Scripture or repeating a title in prayer. It is about knowing Him intimately, knowing that you are a part of Him and He is a part of you. It is living with the assurance that He cares about every detail of your life, even your dating life. He loves you completely right now, and there is nothing you can do to make Him love you more than He does right now.

To know Him is to love Him. It means wanting Him, not just needing Him. As Father, He is tender yet strong, a listener who hears your every word, a guide who corrects you without making you feel abandoned. He is available. He is reliable. And when you live in that kind of intimacy with Him, it changes everything.

It gives you a confidence that is unshakable, the kind of confidence that makes you, as a daughter, laugh at the future like the Proverbs 31 woman. It helps you look in the mirror and see yourself the way He sees you, beautiful even with your flaws. It teaches you to respect yourself in ways you never have before. As you learn to love God in a healthy way, you begin to love yourself in a healthy way. And only then can you love others the way Jesus calls us to.

That kind of love shifts how you see your season of singleness. It takes the weight off the "when" and places it back on the "Who."

...

Reflection

Before you continue, pause to sit with what this chapter stirred in you. Becoming a daughter before becoming a bride requires unlearning some deep habits of striving and learning to rest in being loved. These questions are meant to help you slow down and listen—not perform. Let them draw you closer to the Father who already delights in you.

1. *How would you describe your current relationship with God as Father?*
2. *In what areas of your life would intimacy with Him give you more confidence?*
3. *How might seeing yourself the way God sees you change the way you date, pursue purpose, or make decisions in this season?*

5 | The Weight of "When"

There was a season I genuinely believed marriage had somehow evaded me—that maybe I had missed the mark or wasn't good enough. Maybe God was punishing me for my past. And if you've ever been in that place, you know how heavy the wait can feel.

Psalm 27:14 offers a different perspective: *"Wait for the Lord; be strong and take heart and wait for the Lord"* (Psalm 27:14 NIV). The Hebrew word for "wait" here, *qavah*, means to actively look for, to hope with expectation, to entwine your heart with God's while you anticipate what He is doing (Strong's H6960). Waiting on God is about seeking Him, trusting His character, and aligning with His will.

But I wasn't doing that. I wasn't truly waiting *on God*: I was waiting *for a husband*. I had fixed my eyes on the thing more than on the One, and idolatry slowly crept in. It hid under hope and quietly shifted my worship from God to the gift He wanted to give.

Seeking His Hand, Not His Heart

The longer I "waited" on God, the more weight I began to feel. And the longer I carried the weight, the more it revealed the ugliness in my heart. I realized I wasn't seeking God for who He is. I was seeking Him for what I wanted Him to give me.

It didn't start that way. In the beginning, my pursuit of Him was genuine. I read my Bible because I was hungry for truth. I prayed because I wanted to hear His voice. I worshiped because I loved Him. But slowly, without even noticing, my motives shifted.

I started reading Scripture like it was a treasure map to my husband. I prayed less to know God's will and more to get His "yes." My worship became spiritual bargaining. My obedience became a checklist. And my joy started to fade, because no matter how much I did, nothing seemed to change.

I was still single.

I prayed, fasted, asked for signs, and convinced myself the "peace" I felt meant divine approval for every step I took. And for a season, it seemed like God's blessing was on it. But once I stopped seeking His direction and started scripting my own, the peace turned into pressure. The joy turned into obsession. And the clarity I thought I had blurred into confusion.

Looking back, I see it now:
I was chasing His hand, not His heart.

And when your pursuit shifts like that, it always comes with a cost. The longer I stayed in that place, the heavier the weight became: until it started to shape not just my choices, but the way I thought about myself, my worth, and my future.

Have you ever realized your prayers were more about outcomes than intimacy?

The Emotional Toll

When clarity turned into confusion, it wasn't just my own thoughts I had to wrestle with. The outside voices didn't make it any easier. Well-meaning family members. Curious friends. Even strangers with unsolicited advice. Their questions came like clockwork:

"Why are you still single? Do you want kids? Do you want to get married?"

And when you're over thirty, those questions carry more weight. The stigma sinks deeper. Society starts whispering, *"If you were really whole, you wouldn't still be single. Something must be wrong with you."*

Eventually, those whispers found their way into my own heart. I started to think of marriage like a lifetime achievement award, and the wedding was the lavish ceremony where I'd finally be rewarded for surviving this waiting. Marriage felt like an exclusive club I kept getting left out of. And the longer I waited, the more I started to believe something was wrong with me.

I hated that I felt this way. I tried to fight the thoughts, but sometimes, they won.

No, I'm not desperate—but what if I am?

No, I'm not lonely—but what if I'm tired of being alone?
No, I'm not jealous—but why does it feel like everyone
else gets what I've been praying for?

The battle was relentless. And the more I wrestled with those questions, the more I wore myself down. Eventually, I burned out. I started dating for all the wrong reasons — validation, distraction, performance, escape. The wait had drained me. I wasn't just exhausted emotionally; I was exhausted spiritually. I had made marriage the goal, and in chasing it, I was losing myself.

I didn't know it then, but exhaustion often comes right before exposure: the moment when God reveals what your heart has truly been chasing.

A Yes Without His Process

When I started dating my ex-husband, the joy came rushing back. It felt like the waiting had paid off. I believed he was the man God had confirmed for me—and to this day, I still believe that confirmation was real. But here's where I went wrong: I didn't wait for God's full instructions on how He wanted us to proceed. I took the "yes" and started writing the rest of the story myself.

Looking back, I understand now that divine confirmation isn't divine automation.

This is important, because a lot of people assume failed relationships mean the man was never approved by God in the first place. Sometimes that's true. But in my case, it

Page | 39

wasn't. The real problem was free will. My choices turned a "yes" into confusion. I rushed ahead, moved faster than His timing, and leaned on my own understanding. And any time we try to make God fit into our script instead of surrendering to His, chaos is inevitable.

A lot of believers struggle with this same tension. We want God to give us a yes, but we don't always wait for His process. And when it comes to marriage, we treat free will differently than in any other area of life. We'll make career moves, financial decisions, even parenting choices with full ownership and responsibility.

But with marriage, it's as if some of us expect God to play magician: to drop the right man in front of us without our participation, without our discernment, and without our accountability. That mindset not only takes away ownership; it also distorts how we see God. And when you mix impatience with misplaced expectations, you end up doing what Abraham and Sarah once did in Genesis: birthing Ishmael when God had already promised Isaac.

The Ishmael vs. Isaac Moment

When I look back on that season of my life, I can't help but think of Abraham and Sarah. God had already promised them a son, but waiting was not easy. They were both way beyond the age of procreating children, so the very thought of being parents at that age didn't make sense to them. Year after year went by, the ticking of time grew louder than the sound of God's promise, so they did what many of us have done—they made their own plan. Sarah convinced Abraham to have a baby with Hagar, and he agreed. The result was Ishmael (See Genesis 16).

But here's the thing: Ishmael wasn't the fulfillment of God's word. He was the product of impatience. Isaac was still the promise.

This story isn't just familiar to me because I've read it. I lived my own version of it. Before I ever met my ex-husband, I truly believe the Lord confirmed that I would marry: that my husband would be humble, that he'd complement me, that together we would build a life with Him at the center. When I met my ex, I received further confirmation in multiple ways and even through different people in our lives. But like Abraham and Sarah, I took the promise and ran ahead of God. We thought His yes meant we could hit fast-forward, when what we really needed to do was pause.

The problem was, once we believed we had a "yes" from God, we stopped seeking His instructions. Instead of asking *how* and *when* He wanted us to move forward, we decided to write the script ourselves. One of those self-written chapters was moving in together after only a few months of dating, something I'll unpack more in the chapter *Saints and Situationships*. The choice alone planted us on a shaky foundation that only grew harder to balance.

From there, it felt like a see-saw: moments of surrender followed by moments of taking control again. Confirmation had turned into confusion, and our free will choices pulled us further and further from the original path God had laid out.

Here's what I discovered: God's yes doesn't excuse us from His process. When we step outside of that process, we risk birthing Ishmael— something that looks like a blessing but carries the weight of striving, instability, and pain.

And yet, the grace of God is that even when we create Ishmaels, His promise still stands. Isaac is still the promise. His word does not change, even if our choices take us on detours.

And here is the beauty: God didn't curse Ishmael. In fact, He blessed him and promised to make him into a great nation, even though Ishmael wasn't part of His original plan. But notice this: that blessing came after Hagar surrendered to God in the wilderness and after Abraham and Sarah faced the weight of their choices. There had to be conviction and surrender before God stepped in. It's not that He couldn't fix it without them; relationship with God requires partnership. Free will means we participate in His plans. That's why surrender is key. We cannot keep our hands on the mess and expect Him to clean it up on our terms. But when we take our hands off and give it back to Him, He redeems it. Our Ishmaels may carry consequences, but they are never beyond His correction or His grace.

What I Missed Before Marriage

Waiting wasn't my problem. How I waited was. I thought the goal was marriage, but God was trying to show me that the real goal was maturity. Learning to surrender, to walk with Him, to trust His timing and His process. And part of that process wasn't just about romance. It was about relationship. The kind that sharpens you, strengthens you, and stretches you long before a wedding day ever arrives. The truth is, I would have saved myself a lot of heartbreak if I had learned the value of Godly friendships, especially with men, before I ever called someone "boyfriend" or "husband." Marriage was never meant to be the training ground for learning how to love people well—friendship is. And that's where we're headed next.

...

Reflection

Before we move forward, pause here for a moment of reflection. The waiting season has a way of exposing what's really in our hearts: our fears, our desires, even our impatience. But it's also an invitation to step back and consider what God might be after—not just your future marriage, but your present maturity. Use the questions to check in with yourself before we continue.

1. In your own waiting season, have you confused "seeking God" with seeking what He could give you? What did that look like in practice?
2. How have impatience or free will choices—rushing ahead of God's process—shaped your relationships or outlook on love?

3. When you think about surrender, what areas of your heart or life do you still struggle to fully hand over to God?

6| Brothers Before Boaz

Somewhere along the way, "just friends" became Christian code for failure, as if it meant you didn't make the cut for romance. But God never treated friendship as a downgrade. In fact, some of the most powerful relationships in Scripture weren't marriages at all. They were friendships. The kind that carried covenants, sharpened character, and revealed what real love looks like. And when I say covenant, I don't just mean a fancy Bible word. A covenant is a sacred commitment, deeper than feelings and stronger than convenience. It's a bond marked by loyalty, sacrifice, and intentional love.

If we learned how to value friendship the way God does, we'd save ourselves from a lot of heartbreak. Because friendship is where you learn loyalty. It's where you practice vulnerability. It's where you practice grace and forgiveness. And it's where you discover who shows up when life gets heavy. Romance may get the spotlight, but friendship is where the real work happens.

And the best part? Those same lessons you learn in friendship are the very ones that hold marriages together.

We're going to look at why friendship matters more than you think. First, through the lens of same-sex friendships like Ruth and Naomi, and Jonathan and David. Finally, we'll begin unpacking what Godly platonic friendships with the opposite sex can teach us about discernment and maturity.

Ruth and Naomi:
Loyalty Before Boaz

Christian culture has reduced Ruth's life to a love story with Boaz. But long before Boaz ever stepped onto the scene, there was Naomi. Their bond wasn't a filler while Ruth waited for something "better." It was a covenant. It was loyalty that redefined what real friendship looks like.

We already looked at Ruth 1:16-17 earlier in this book, where Ruth declared she would go wherever Naomi went, live wherever she lived, and worship Naomi's God as her own. That wasn't about preparing for marriage. It wasn't even about a man. It was about commitment, faithfulness, and showing up when it would have been easier to walk away.

And here's the thing: Ruth's loyalty didn't just benefit Naomi. It shaped Ruth, too. Her faithfulness positioned her to step into God's bigger plan, but it wasn't a strategy to "get a husband." It was simply who she was choosing to be: a faithful friend.

That's what makes their relationship so powerful for us today. Friendship isn't a stepping stone into something greater. Friendship *is* great. It's the foundation of every other relationship we will ever have—including marriage if that's in our story, but also in family, ministry, and community. Ruth and Naomi remind us that covenant-level friendships aren't optional extras; they are part of how God builds us, strengthens us, and prepares us for whatever He has called us to do.

Ruth's loyalty showed us covenant in action; Jonathan's loyalty shows us what covenant looks like in conflict.

Jonathan and David:
A Brother Like No Other

One of the most radical examples of loyalty in Scripture is the friendship of Jonathan and David (See 1 Samuel, Chapters 18-23). By birthright, Jonathan should have been next in line to be king. But God had chosen David instead. To make matters even more complicated, Jonathan's father, King Saul, loved David at first. David was the young warrior who defeated the giant, Goliath, when no one else would step up. Saul welcomed him into the palace and celebrated him, until jealousy crept in and love turned to rage. Saul went from loving David to trying to kill him. If anyone had a motive to hate David, it was Jonathan. David was the man standing in the way of his future and the one his father wanted dead.

But Jonathan didn't let jealousy or pressure from his father define him. He chose covenant over competition. He saw David's character, he knew God's hand was on his life, and instead of resenting him, he protected him. He warned David when Saul was plotting against him. He defended him when Saul tried to slander him. He even risked his own safety to help David escape when his father's rage got out of control.

That kind of friendship is rare. Most people would've sided with family, allowed bitterness to creep in, or protected their own interests. Jonathan did the hard thing. He laid down ambition, pride, and even his own future for the sake of friendship.

And this is the lesson for us. Real friendship isn't tested when everything is easy; it's tested when envy, comparison, or outside voices try to creep in. Jonathan and David show us that true friendship requires courage, sacrifice, and trust. If Jonathan could love and protect the very man who took what was "rightfully" his, then we can learn to put ego aside for the people God calls us to walk with.

Scripture Over Culture

We live in a culture that has watered friendship down to hashtags and highlight reels. Same-sex friendship often gets reduced to "bestie" culture: all selfies, vacations, and birthday brunches, but not much depth beyond the photo ops. And when it comes to opposite-sex friendships, forget it. Many people—even in church spaces—still believe the idea that men and women can't really be friends without it turning romantic or messy.

But the Bible paints a very different picture. John 15:12-15 (NIV) sets the tone by showing us that friendship isn't surface level at all. It's sacrificial. Jesus said, "Greater love has no one than this: to lay down one's life for one's friends." That means real love doesn't just hang out when it's convenient; it's willing to bleed for someone else.

Have you ever had a friend whose loyalty cost them something? Have you ever been that friend?

Proverbs 17:17 (NIV)takes it a step further: *"A friend loves at all times."* Not sometimes, not when it feels good, not when it benefits you—all times. The kind of consistency that doesn't ghost you when things get hard is rare, but that's the kind of friendship God calls us to.

And then, there's Ecclesiastes 4:9-10 (NIV), which paints this vivid picture: *"Two are better than one...If either of them falls down, one can help the other up."* That's not a wedding verse; it's a life verse. God designed us to need people who will reach down and pull us back up when we fall.

Finally, Galatians 6:2 (NIV) drives it home with a challenge: *"Carry each other's burdens."* Real friendship isn't just inside jokes and road trips. It's stepping into someone else's struggle and saying, "I'll help you hold this."

None of these are gender-specific. They're kingdom principles. Whether it's a sisterhood that grounds you or a brother in Christ who sharpens you, God has given us the blueprint for friendship that lasts.

And this matters, because when we don't know what friendship is supposed to look like, we start confusing it with everything: attraction, attention, or even performance. That's what happened to me. I didn't know how to simply be someone's friend, and it cost me.

The Friendship Fumble

There was a time in college when I met a guy who shared several of my classes, and we instantly vibed. We had so much in common: same faith, similar humor, deep conversations, and a natural ease when we were around each other. I genuinely felt safe with him. But because I had never learned how to build a platonic friendship with a man, my feelings quickly turned romantic.

Without realizing it, I began to pursue him emotionally. I overcompensated by being overly generous, doing favors, trying to impress him, and subtly dropping hints that I wanted something more. What could have been a beautiful, God-ordained friendship turned into awkward encounters, strained conversations, and ultimately distance.

Looking back, I see now that I pushed away an amazing friend simply because I didn't understand the value of "just friends." At the time, only being friends sounded like rejection. When in reality, it could have been the very foundation for something more meaningful: biblical friendship.

When cultivated the right way, friendship can become the soil where Godly relationships grow. But here's the hard question: how many of us have fumbled a friendship because we didn't value it for what it was? Maybe you turned distance into drama. Maybe you let insecurity or hidden motives get in the way. Or maybe you simply didn't pour into the friendship the way you should have.

Those moments matter, because friendship is the training ground for every other relationship you'll ever build, including romance.

The Practice Before the Promise

Unhealthy friendship patterns almost always spill over into poor dating habits. If you don't know how to handle conflict with a friend, dating won't miraculously fix that. If you don't know how to serve without keeping score, marriage won't suddenly make you selfless. If you can't sit and truly listen in friendship, you won't turn into a great communicator just because you put "girlfriend" in your bio.

Think about it. The friend who can't keep your confidence probably won't protect your heart in romance. The one who disappears when things get hard won't stick around when marriage gets heavy. The person who always takes but never gives won't transform into a selfless partner just because feelings are involved.

This is why friendship matters more than we give it credit for. Romance doesn't transform someone's character— it reveals it. And if you haven't learned how to love well as a friend, you're going to stumble as a girlfriend, fiancée, or wife.

This is also why discernment in dating starts here. Before you ever step into romance, friendship teaches you how to recognize red flags, pay attention to patterns, and notice how someone treats people when no feelings are on the line. Later, in the chapter *Dating with Discernment,* we'll dive deeper into how this plays out in relationships. But for now, understand this: friendship is your classroom, and if you skip class, don't expect to ace the test.

You Say He's Just a Friend...

Here's the truth: men and women *can* be friends. But healthy friendships don't just happen by accident. They're built on boundaries, clarity, and intention.

Boundaries protect the friendship from confusion. It's not about building walls; it's about creating safety. That may look like being honest about your intentions, setting limits on how much one-on-one time you spend, or choosing group settings when emotions feel murky. Clear boundaries protect both hearts and keep motives from getting twisted.

Clarity is equally important. Not every text needs to feel like a marriage interview, but it's wise to define the friendship when needed. Sometimes the most Godly thing you can say is, "I value you as a friend, and I want to keep it that way." That kind of honesty prevents unnecessary pain down the road.

And then there's intention. You don't have to over-spiritualize every hangout or Bible study, but you should ask yourself: What's the fruit of this friendship? Does it push me closer to Christ? Does it sharpen my discernment? Does it reflect respect? Godly friendships are meant to strengthen your character, not confuse your calling.

The beauty is this: cultivating friendships with men in safe, platonic ways sharpens your discernment. You begin to recognize who is trustworthy and who is not. You start to see the difference between charm and character. You learn what covenant love looks like in a non-romantic space, which makes it easier to recognize it when God does lead you into romance.

Friendship has a way of revealing the truth about us: what we value, how we handle conflict, and whether we're capable of showing up for someone else. If we pay attention, it teaches us lessons that romance alone could never teach. And that's the point. The same wisdom that strengthens our friendships is the wisdom we carry into dating.

Before we talk about what it means to date with discernment, pause and let this sink in: how you love your friends is shaping the way you will love anyone else. And if you let God guide you here, you'll already be walking in the kind of clarity that makes dating less confusing and far more intentional.

...

Reflection

Before we turn the page to talk about dating, take a moment to sit with this. Friendship is often where God does His deepest work in us—sharpening our character, stretching our patience, and teaching us how to love without conditions. These questions are not about shame; they're about awareness. Let them guide you into honest reflection.

1. *Have I treated friendship as less valuable than romance? If so, what has it cost me?*
2. *What patterns in my friendships— loyalty, conflict, consistency, or boundaries—reveal how I might show up in dating?*
3. *How can I begin cultivating healthier friendships, with both women and men, that reflect the kind of covenant love God calls me to?*

7| Holy, Not Helpless: Dating with Discernment

For a long time, I believed that God was going to hand-deliver my husband. I believed if I stayed patient, focused on "becoming the one," and stayed out of the dating scene, the man He chose for me would show up right on time. No apps. No awkward conversations. No effort. Just divine delivery.

But here's what I had to learn: God cares deeply about who we partner with, but He doesn't usually drop people out of the sky—even though He absolutely could. He rarely overrides our free will. Instead, He invites us to walk with Him in the process. He gives us wisdom, discernment, and the Holy Spirit to guide our steps. The Bible says He *orders our steps* (Psalm 37:23), not drags us down the aisle.

We aren't called to sit passively and hope the perfect man appears at our doorstep. We're called to walk with God, stay aligned with Him, and make decisions with His counsel. Dating is one of those decisions. And when done with discernment, it can be holy, intentional, and even fun. But if we approach it with fear, fantasy, or false ideas of how God works, we'll stay stuck waiting for a love story He's inviting us to co-write with Him.

What the Bible Says
(and Doesn't Say) About Dating

The Bible doesn't give us a playbook on dating. There's no verse that says, "Thou shalt text back within 3 hours," or "Swipe left until you find a man of God." Dating didn't exist in biblical times, but that doesn't mean God left us without direction. He gave us principles, and one of the clearest ones comes straight out of Romans 12:2:

"Do not conform to the pattern of this world but be transformed by the renewing of your mind. Then you will be able to test and approve what God's will is — His good, pleasing and perfect will" (Romans 12:2 NIV).

That one verse is a whole framework for how to approach Christian life, especially relationships.

The first part says, *do not conform to the pattern of this world*. This includes cycles, lifestyles, and mindsets. And let's be honest, the world has a lot of patterns when it comes to dating: hook-up culture, situationships, playing games, and even some of the unhealthy Christian subculture habits we've picked up along the way. (Don't worry, we'll talk more about those in *Saints and Situationships*.)

The second part says, *be transformed by the renewing of your mind*. For us as believers, renewing our mind isn't just about positive thinking. It's about gaining Godly knowledge through His word, applying that knowledge with wisdom, and pairing it with understanding. Transformation starts in the mind before it ever shows up in our dating habits.

Then comes the promise: *then you will be able to test and approve what God's will is.* That's how discernment is built. What qualifies us to know God's will isn't wishful thinking, it's allowing Him to reshape our mindset, our cycles, and our patterns until they reflect His.

This is why Romans 12:2 is so important when we talk about dating. It forces us to stop and ask:

- *Am I approaching this relationship God's way or the world's way?*
- *Have I adopted behaviors that feel normal but aren't Christ-like?*
- *Am I renewing my mind, or just recycling patterns?*

When you start to analyze your dating life through that lens, clarity comes quickly: sometimes uncomfortably so.

In the Beginning

When we look at Genesis 2, the creation of Adam and Eve, it wasn't a scene from a romantic movie. It was purposeful. God created the Garden of Eden, and it needed to be cared for. He placed Adam in the garden to work, to name the animals, and to walk with Him. Adam wasn't sitting around praying for a wife or begging for companionship. He didn't even know he had a need. It was God who looked at Adam's situation and said, *"It's not good for man to be alone"* (Genesis 2:18 NIV).

And notice what God said. He didn't say Adam needed a girlfriend. He said Adam needed a *helper* suitable for him. The word "helper" wasn't about someone to sit pretty in the garden. It was about someone who could walk with Adam in his assignment and multiply the impact of what God had already placed in his hands.

The story has been romanticized and preached at weddings for years, but at its core, it's not about romance. It's about responsibility. Marriage wasn't designed to soothe loneliness, check off a life goal, or give Adam a legal way to have sex. It was designed with a mission in mind: to glorify God and to steward His creation. And that truth applies to any relationship God ordains.

Restoring the Blueprint:
What Ephesians 5 Really Teaches Us

Now that we understand the *why* of marriage from Genesis, let's talk about the *how*. Ephesians 5:21-33 is one of the most quoted passages about marriage, but it's also one of the most misused. Too many of us have heard it twisted into control tactics, half-truths, or outdated gender wars. But when you read it through God's heart, it gives us a beautiful picture of what covenant is supposed to look like. (Ephesians 5:21–33 NIV).

Verse 21:
"Submit to one another out of reverence for Christ."

This is where it starts: not with hierarchy, but humility. Both husband and wife first submit to God, and out of that posture, they submit to each other. Mutual submission is the foundation. It's not about who's in charge, it's about both being surrendered to Christ.

Verses 22-24:

"Wives, submit yourselves to your own husbands as you do to the Lord...as the church submits to Christ, so also wives should submit to their husbands in everything."

This is the part that gets weaponized the most. But biblical submission is not about silence or oppression. It's about trust. It's the same kind of willing surrender we already practice with Christ: a choice, not a command forced on us. And notice, Paul doesn't say women submit to *all men*. He says submit to your own husband. That's covenant language.

Verse 25:

"Husbands, love your wives, just as Christ loved the church and gave Himself up for her."

This is the real weight of leadership. If a man isn't willing to die to himself daily— his pride, his convenience, his ego— then he's not leading like Christ. Headship isn't about control. It's about sacrifice.

What would it look like to be loved like that: not with control, but with sacrifice?

Verses 26-27:

"...to make her holy, cleansing her by the washing with water through the word, and to present her to himself as a radiant church..."

This shows us what spiritual covering looks like. A Godly husband doesn't just provide; he cultivates. He brings God's Word into the home, prays with and for his wife, and creates a space where she can flourish in her calling. He doesn't compete with her. He covers her.

Verses 28-30:

"In the same way, husbands ought to love their wives as their own bodies…"

Paul makes it practical here. Just like we take care of our own bodies, a husband is called to care for his wife's whole well-being: physical, emotional, spiritual. Love means nurture, not neglect.

Verses 31-32:

"'For this reason a man will leave his father and mother and be united to his wife, and the two will become flesh.'
This is profound mystery,
but I am talking about Christ and the church."

This is why marriage is sacred. It's not just about two people building a life together: it mirrors Christ's covenant with His church. That's why discernment matters so much before you say "I do." You're stepping into something that reflects God's eternal plan.

Verse 33:

"Each of one of you also must love his wife as he loves himself, and the wife must respect her husband."

Paul sums it up here. When love and respect flow freely on both sides, the relationship thrives. A man who feels respected loves well. A woman who feels loved respects deeply. It's mutual.

Ephesians 5 isn't about domination or passivity. It's about partnership that mirrors Christ and His church. It's about sacrificial love, mutual honor, and spiritual responsibility. This is the standard God gave us for marriage, so why would we treat dating like it's anything less?

Once you see what covenant love looks like, the question becomes: how do we date in a way that honors that same design?

Courtship, Dating, or Something in Between?

Nobody in the Bible dated the way we do today. In biblical times, marriages were arranged by families, shaped by cultural customs, and confirmed through community involvement. There were no dating apps, no "talking stage," and no awkward texting games. Fast forward to now, and Christians are stuck trying to navigate a system the Bible doesn't outline, which is why we have to be careful about which model we follow.

Here's the truth: **worldly dating and courtship are not the same.**

- **Worldly dating** is casual, undefined, and without boundaries. It's often driven by feelings, chemistry, and convenience. It looks just like the world because that's where it comes from. No accountability. No clear purpose. No guardrails. And honestly, this is where most situationships are born (which we'll discuss in more detail later).

- **Courtship,** on the other hand, is intentional. It invites God, mentors, and community into the process. It's dating with clarity, accountability, and the clear purpose of evaluating someone for marriage. Courtship doesn't mean you have to marry the first person you sit across from at a coffee shop. It means you know why you're dating, who's speaking into your life, and what boundaries keep you aligned with God's design.

I'm not saying you have to call it "courtship" to do it God's way. Some people say they're "dating" but live out courtship principles. That's fine. What matters isn't the label, it's the lifestyle.

Are you dating with accountability? Are you honoring God with your body and emotions? Are you walking in community instead of secrecy? If not, you're not practicing Godly dating. You're practicing the world's version.

So, from here on out, when I use the word *dating*, I'm not talking about the world's version. I'm talking about dating with courtship principles: intentional, accountable, and covenant-minded. You don't have to call it "courtship" if that word feels outdated, but you do need to live by its standards if you want God's best.

Don't Skip the Friend Zone

We already talked back in Chapter 6 about why friendship matters. And when you skip it, the cost shows up later. I learned that the hard way.

One of the biggest cracks in my marriage foundation was that I rushed past friendship. I jumped straight into romance, assuming chemistry and confirmation was enough. At the time, I thought I was being obedient. I was praying, fasting, journaling, doing all the "right" things. But skipping friendship meant I missed the chance to see gaps that attraction alone couldn't cover. Friendship would've slowed me down, forced harder questions, and shown me whether we could walk in purpose together before ever saying "I do".

I'll share more about how that choice led me down a path I wish I'd avoided in the next chapter. For now, I just want you to know this: the friend zone isn't punishment. It's protection. And skipping it will cost more than you think.

Start How You Mean to Stay

The beginning always sets the tone. How you start a relationship is how you'll end up sustaining it. If you build it on clarity, boundaries, and purpose, you'll have something that can stand. If you build it on assumptions, excuses, or compromise, you'll spend the whole time trying to fix cracks that could've been avoided.

I know, because I lived it. Skipping friendship and rushing into romance felt good in the moment, but it laid a shaky foundation. What I ignored at the start became the very things that unraveled me later. Hear my heart, Sis: you cannot start sloppy and expect to end holy.

So how do you start strong? It comes down to three things:

Honesty. From the beginning, honesty sets the tone. That doesn't mean trauma-dumping your life story on the first date, but it does mean being clear about who you are and what you're looking for. Mixed signals create mixed outcomes. If you know you're dating with the hope of marriage, don't pretend you're fine with casual just to keep someone interested.

Boundaries. Boundaries aren't about limiting fun; they're about protecting what matters most. Clear emotional, physical, and even digital boundaries create safety for both people. Someone who respects your boundaries is showing you they can respect you. Someone who won't is already showing you the opposite.

Purpose Alignment. This is where discernment steps in. Early on, pay attention to whether your values and assignments line up. You don't need to have the same career path or personality, but you do need the same foundation in Christ and a willingness to pursue Him together. If your purpose is to glorify God in your calling, but his is still undefined or running in the opposite direction, don't ignore that. Alignment matters more than chemistry.

When these three things are set early, it doesn't take long for someone's true colors to show. Either they rise to meet the standard, or the cracks start showing. And that's where truth comes into focus, showing you whether you're building toward covenant or chaos.

Flags Don't Lie

Starting strong is one thing, but staying strong is another. The way someone shows up over time will reveal whether they're building with you or just playing with your heart. Wisdom in dating isn't just about spotting red flags. It's also about recognizing the green ones. We often ask God to expose what's wrong with a man, but do we ask Him to confirm what's right?

After disappointment or deception, it's easy to obsess over what you don't want. But when your heart is healed and your vision clear, you'll notice the fruit of the Spirit in someone's life— not just their church attendance or social media Bible quotes. And let's be clear: just because someone goes to church doesn't mean they're submitted to Christ. The truth will always come out in how he lives, not just in what he says.

Green Flags:
Signs of Spiritual Maturity

- **Submitted to God's Authority.** Not just a believer in name, but a man who fears the Lord. He applies the Word, not just quotes it. Watch how he handles conflict, money, repentance, and leadership. The fruit is in the follow-through.

- **Seeks wise counsel.** He doesn't live in isolation. He invites mentors, pastors, and Godly friends to speak into his life. Accountability is humility in action.
- **Emotionally mature.** He listens without defensiveness, owns his mistakes, and talks through conflict without gaslighting, manipulation, or deflecting.
- **Respects boundaries.** A man who honors your no shows he can practice self-control. If he respects you here, he'll respect you everywhere.
- **Consistent.** Not perfect, but steady. His actions match his words, and you don't have to guess where you stand with him.
- **Points you back to Christ.** After time with him, do you feel anchored in God or distracted by fantasy? A Godly man adds focus to your faith, not confusion to your heart.

Red Alerts:
Spiritually Dressed, Flesh-Led

- **Uses God to manipulate.** "God told me you're my wife" might sound spiritual but it often masks immaturity or control. Pause, pray, and seek clarity before you buy into it.

- **Talks God, walks flesh.** A dinner prayer means nothing if his life shows no conviction, no service, and no respect for women.
- **Rushes intimacy.** Whether emotional or physical, if he wants speed without commitment, that's not divine acceleration. That's immaturity.
- **No spiritual community.** If no one can vouch for him, challenge him, or hold him accountable, that's isolation. And isolation breeds danger.
- **No sense of purpose.** A man who doesn't know where he's going isn't ready to lead. Purpose brings clarity; confusion only multiplies chaos.
- **Treats dating like a game.** Mixed signals, ghosting, flirting with boundaries...that's playboy behavior dressed in church clothes.

At the end of the day, Sis, green flags and red alerts aren't about spotting "the one." They're survival tools. They guard your heart while keeping it open to what God has for you. You don't need perfection, you need patterns. And once your vision clears, you won't have to chase clarity: it will meet you, and peace will follow.

Wisdom Over Wasted Time

Here's the gift of discernment: it doesn't just tell you who to avoid, it protects your time, your peace, and your heart. When you invite God into the process, you start recognizing patterns early instead of ignoring red alerts and hoping they'll go away.

God's wisdom saves you from pouring years into someone who was never aligned with your purpose. It protects you from attaching your heart to a man who can quote Scripture but won't live it. It keeps you from mistaking chemistry for covenant. That same wisdom also holds you accountable to keeping a pure heart posture, too.

But God's guidance doesn't just guard you from the wrong ones. It also opens your eyes to the right things. Peace that isn't forced. Respect that isn't demanded. Consistency that doesn't have to be begged for.

When you walk closely with Him, you stop wasting energy chasing what looks good and start investing in what is truly good. This isn't about being suspicious of everyone you meet. It's about learning to lean into His Spirit so that truth rises to the surface long before your emotions can trick you.

That's how heartbreak loses power. That's how wasted time becomes a testimony instead of a pattern.

...

Reflection

Dating with God isn't about finding a flawless formula. It's about learning to walk in wisdom so your heart, your time, and your peace are protected. Before you step into the next chapter, pause and consider these questions for yourself.

1. *Have I invited God into my dating life in a way that brings clarity, or am I still waiting passively for Him to do all the work?*

2.	*Which patterns — honesty, boundaries, alignment — have I overlooked in past relationships, and how can I protect them moving forward?*
3.	*Am I willing to trust God's wisdom to show me both the green lights I can pursue and the red alerts I need to walk away from?*

8| Saints and Situationships

We all know what commitment looks like. And we know what casual looks like. But somewhere in between is the space a lot of us get stuck in: *the situationship.*

A situationship is a relationship that looks like dating but never fully becomes it. The titles are blurry, the boundaries are shaky, and the future is undefined. It's connection without clarity, intimacy without commitment, and just enough attention to keep you hanging on. And sadly, it's not just a cultural problem. Even in the church, too many of us are settling for half-love because it feels easier than waiting on the real thing. And if our dating looks the same as the world's, it means a mindset somewhere is not renewed.

Here's the problem: Christians are supposed to be set apart, but too often the way we date doesn't look any different than the world. If someone compared two believers on a date with two non-believers, they'd struggle to see a difference. Same patterns. Same conversations. Same lack of standards. And that's because we've conformed. We binge the world's dating shows, copy its books and podcasts, and recycle its advice without ever weighing it against the Word of God.

Paul reminds us in Romans 12 that we can't copy the world's patterns and expect Godly results. A renewed mind recognizes God's will, including in dating. Dating is meant to be a process of testing and approving—discerning whether someone has the character and alignment to walk with you long term. Without a renewed mind, you'll default to the world's way of dating. And that default is what pulls so many of us into situationships.

Half-Love, Whole Mess

A situationship isn't just about not having a title. It's about living in the tension of "almost." Almost a relationship. Almost committed. Almost aligned. It's just enough to keep you invested, but never enough to move forward.

For Christians, it often looks like this: praying without real purpose. Acting like a couple without covenant. Using spiritual language to cover up immaturity. On the surface, it feels like progress. In reality, it's a holding pattern.

So why do we end up here?

- *Sometimes it's fear*: fear of being alone, so we cling to "almost" instead of moving on.
- *Sometimes it's loneliness*: the kind that makes companionship feel more urgent than covenant.
- *Sometimes it's convenience*: because half-love feels easier than risking heartbreak.
- *Sometimes it's validation*: wanting to feel chosen, even if the choice isn't secure. Different

reasons, same result: "almost" keeps you busy while your purpose sits idle.

But here's the cost: half-commitments don't just waste your time. They rewire your heart.

Emotionally, they drain you. They keep you questioning your worth with, *"What are we? Where is this going?"* They stir up insecurity because you're always trying to earn clarity that should've been there from the start.

Spiritually, they distract you. You start treating "almost" like a blessing, when it's really a counterfeit. False intimacy blurs your discernment and numbs your conviction. You pray for direction, but your actions contradict the prayers.

Relationally, they break you down. Boundaries blur, cycles of starting and stopping wear you out, and the healing you'll need when it finally ends is deeper than you expected. Half-commitments leave scars because they ask you to invest like a covenant while withholding the covering of one.

Half-commitments sound harmless until you live one. I know, because I did. I told myself good intentions, prayer, and love would be enough to make "almost" feel holy. But half-love doesn't transform into covenant just because you sprinkle faith on top. What felt like progress was really compromise dressed up as purpose. And nowhere was that clearer than when I prematurely moved in with the man who later became my husband.

When Close Enough Isn't Good Enough

I never meant to rush. I honestly believed I was being obedient. When I met my ex-husband, I felt a nudge from the Holy Spirit, a quiet confirmation that he would one day be my husband. I wasn't looking for a casual connection. I was praying, fasting, journaling: doing all the "right" things. So when I felt a peace about him, I took that as a green light to move forward...fast.

But fast turned into foolishness. What started out as intentional dating slowly slid into prematurely "playing house."

We moved in together and dressed it up as getting ready for marriage. But it was disobedience in disguise. Shortly after, things began to unravel. The spiritual connection faded. Confusion crept in. My spirit felt heavy. I told myself we were building something holy, but the truth? I was building on assumption, not instruction.

And here's what I learned the hard way: "Almost" isn't harmless. It's rebellion dressed up in romance.

The Conviction About Cohabitation

About four months into living with my ex-husband—before he became my husband—I started feeling a weight I couldn't shake. I wanted to know why living together was a sin, especially since I'd heard this my entire life sitting in church pews. I wasn't trying to be rebellious. I genuinely wanted clarity.

A few months earlier, I'd gotten into a heated debate with a close friend who warned me not to move in with him because it was "wrong in God's eyes." I didn't argue that it was right, I just pressed her: *Show me where it says that in the Bible.* She couldn't. I brushed it off, but the question stuck. And eventually, it drove me straight to the Source.

I went to God and asked:

"Why is living together a sin? Is it just because of sex? What if we stop sleeping together and sleep in separate rooms? Would it still be wrong?"

Almost instantly, the Holy Spirit brought a scripture to mind.

"A man leaves his father and mother and cleaves to his wife."

I pulled out my phone and searched it. Matthew 19:5-6 lit up my screen:

"For this reason a man will leave his father and mother and be united to his wife, and the two will become one flesh. So they are no longer two, but one flesh. Therefore, what God has joined together, let no one separate." Matthew 19:5–6 KJV).

At first, I didn't get it. I'd heard that verse a hundred times. It sounded like a pretty wedding day passage, but what did it have to do with cohabiting?

And then I heard the Holy Spirit whisper:

"Read it again."

I read it out loud, and this time it hit different.

Closeness is not covenant.

If leaving, cleaving, and being in covenant is God's definition of marriage, then anything short of that is a counterfeit.

Cohabiting was close. Too close. Close enough that most people on the outside couldn't tell the difference. But that was the problem. It looked like the real thing, but it wasn't God-ordained.

Side note: Before anyone argues Old Testament culture, yes, I know that "knowing" someone often sealed a marriage. But we're also called to follow the laws of the land (Romans 13:1-2). Today, a marriage license is the legal standard. So, if God's Word calls us to covenant and covering, then anything that mimics marriage without submission to that covenant is not just disobedience. It's deception.

The revelation wrecked me. I loved my boyfriend. I was comfortable. And though I now had spiritual clarity, I didn't make the hard choice to move out. I rationalized it. I told myself engagement was just around the corner. I chose convenience over conviction...and I stayed.

Sis, maybe you're in the same boat. You're not trying to rebel; you're just trying to love. And maybe you're convincing yourself that because you pray together, serve together, or even talk about marriage...it's ok.

The reality is: closeness doesn't equal covenant. God isn't asking for perfection, but He is calling for obedience. And delayed obedience? It's still disobedience.

I know how easy it is to justify it:

"We're going to get married anyway."

"We're saving money."

"This is just temporary."

"We're spiritually married in God's eyes."

I told myself the same things. But eventually I had to ask: *If I have to compromise God's standard for this relationship, is this really what God wants for me?*

And when we justify compromise long enough, it opens the door for something darker. That's when Satan does his best work: in the shadows of "almost." The enemy doesn't always show up as rebellion. He disguises himself in almost-right. In Christian vibes without Christ's covering. In God talk without Godly fruit. In covenant language without covenant living.

Don't let culture, or even church culture, convince you that being "almost married" is safe. You don't need to act married to be chosen. God doesn't bless compromise. He blesses obedience.

Your Life Preaches Louder Than Your Lips

Here's the part we don't always admit: compromise doesn't just affect the couple. It ripples out into the body of Christ. This isn't about being strict. It's about protecting people. Paul writes in Romans 14:13 (NIV): *"Make up your mind not to put any stumbling block or obstacle in the way of a brother or sister."* In other words, freedom without love isn't freedom at all —it's recklessness.

Hear me on this. The sin isn't a man and woman sharing a roof. The deeper issue is manufacturing something that looks like marriage without the covenant God designed to define it. From the beginning, His order was distinct: a man leaves his parents and cleaves to his wife. Singleness, then marriage. Two seasons, not a blurred in-between.

And here's the risk. Even if a couple says they're abstaining, no one is going to believe purity lives behind those walls. And maybe they are abstaining. But what about the next couple who imitates them and doesn't have the strength to abstain? Their fall becomes the fruit of your example. That's what Paul was warning about: when your choice becomes someone else's stumbling block.

This isn't legalism. It's love. Romans 14:21 says, *"It is better not to eat meat or drink wine or do anything that will cause your brother or sister to fall"* (Romans 14:21 NIV). That's not about restriction for the sake of rules. It's about responsibility for the sake of love. Love says, *"I'll lay down what looks permissible to me if it means protecting someone else from falling."*

Sis, this is weighty, but it's also freeing. Because the same Spirit who convicts us also empowers us. You don't carry this responsibility alone. God doesn't just call you higher; He walks with you there. Your obedience isn't just guarding your own heart; it's helping guard the hearts of those coming behind you.

And that's the beauty of it: your life really does preach louder than your lips. And by God's grace, what people see in you can point them to Jesus.

Beyond 'Counterfeits' and 'Kingdom Spouses'

Witness isn't just about how we live in community. It shows up in our relationships too. And this is where we've let culture—and sometimes church culture— feed us shortcuts that sound spiritual but aren't biblical. We've built entire narratives out of catchy labels. If it didn't work out, he was a "counterfeit." If he checks a few boxes and makes us feel seen, he must be our "kingdom spouse." But labeling isn't wisdom. Godly wisdom goes deeper than clichés. It tests fruit, examines the patterns, and asks the harder questions: was this alignment, or was this a lesson?

The Counterfeit Myth

We love to call every failed relationship a "counterfeit." It softens the sting. It makes us feel like we dodged the devil instead of admitting we may have just made a choice that didn't lead to marriage. And sometimes it's true: some men are distractions dressed up as potential.

But not every breakup is a counterfeit. Some men weren't frauds, they just weren't your future. Some were mirrors, exposing wounds you hadn't healed from yet. Some were lessons, teaching you boundaries, patience, or the courage to walk away. And some were simply God's timing at work— a reminder that He's still writing your story.

Labeling every ex as a counterfeit might feel spiritual, but it's lazy discernment. It keeps the focus on how "bad" he was, instead of asking, *God, what were you showing me about me?*

Here's the danger: if every man is a counterfeit, then you don't have to take responsibility for your own choices. You don't have to examine your patterns, your healing, or your prayers. You can just blame the enemy and move on unchanged.

Godly wisdom is more mature than that. It doesn't reduce people to villains. It recognizes that not every relationship is meant to end at the altar, and that's ok. It asks better questions: *Was this connection meant for a season, or was I trying to stretch it into forever?*

Not every man is supposed to audition to be your husband. But that doesn't mean he was the enemy's plot. Sometimes, he was simply God's son who crossed your path for a purpose other than marriage. Whether we glamorize someone as "the one" or demonize them as "the counterfeit," labeling still lets us avoid the real assignment: becoming more like Christ.

The Kingdom Spouse Narrative

In 2025, we've moved from "waiting for Boaz" to the "kingdom spouse" narrative. You've seen it: the prophetic dreams, the YouTube videos, the fasts and prayers focused on a husband God supposedly handpicked just for you. And it sounds spiritual. It feels deep. But if we're honest, it's become a distraction.

Make no mistake: God cares about marriage. He can guide us into covenant. And I believe in prophecy— I believe God speaks through His prophets and uses them to confirm His word. But prophecy was never meant to replace personal discernment or feed obsession. It was meant to point us back to Christ, not keep us fixated on a spouse.

This idea that there's one pre-assigned, heaven-stamped soulmate and all we need to do is sit, fast, and wait for the prophecy to unfold? That's not faith. That's fantasy. And it usually produces obsession, passivity, and disappointment. It's just another way of trying to control the outcome.

On another note: every "nice" or church-going man is not your kingdom spouse. Niceness isn't a fruit. Mannerisms aren't maturity. A Godly marriage isn't built on vibes, visions, or hashtags. It's built on purpose alignment, tested character, and the daily decision to love with Christ at the center.

Marriage is a covenant, not a spell. God doesn't drop husbands out of the sky. He leads you. He shapes you. And He helps you choose wisely with prayer, community, and discernment.

So, if you've been waiting on a prophecy to confirm your future, take heart: you don't need a "kingdom spouse" word to do what God has already equipped you to do. He's given you His Spirit to guide, His Word to anchor, and His people to receive counsel from. That's more than enough.

Whether it's counterfeits or kingdom spouses, the trap is the same: leaning on labels instead of learning wisdom. God's goal isn't for you to master Christian lingo. It's for you to walk in alignment.

It's one thing to call out the labels we've believed. It's another to face the patterns we've repeated. That's where we need to go next.

When You Keep Falling...

We don't usually plan to fall. We plan to do better. We swear this time will be different. We confess, we cry, we journal, we pray. And yet, somehow, we find ourselves right back in the same place: the same temptation, the same compromise, the same regret.

Falling into sin once is hard enough. Falling again and again? That's a weight few of us admit we carry. It feels like failure on repeat. It makes you question your strength, your salvation, even God's patience with you.

But here's the truth that set me free: God sees your struggle, not just your slip. He's not distant, shaking His head in disappointment. Conviction is not rejection. It's an invitation back to the arms of the Father who wants you, not just your performance.

If you've been caught in the cycle of sexual sin, hear me: *You are not dirty.*

You are not disqualified.

You are not beyond redemption.

But you do need to stop minimizing it.

This isn't just about willpower. Sexual sin isn't only physical. It clouds your judgment. It tangles your emotions. It distorts your identity. It opens the door to confusion, shame, and emotional entanglement that choke your identity. That's why it feels so heavy, because it's not just behavior. It's bondage. And bondage only breaks through truth and surrender.

So, stop hiding. Stop making excuses. Stop trying to out-discipline your flesh without depending on the Spirit.

Bring it all to God...again. He already knows the pattern. And He knows the healing path that will set you free. For one woman, it may be therapy. For another, accountability. For someone else, a season of fasting and complete disconnection. Whatever it looks like, God is not afraid of your process.

You don't need to stay stuck in shame. But you do need to stop pretending it's not affecting you.

Freedom is possible. Not through secret cycles. But through complete surrender.

And maybe you're thinking, *"Ok, I've slipped before, but we didn't even have sex. So, it's not that serious, right?"*

Sis...let's talk.

It's Not Sex, But It Ain't Holy Either

The world has mastered the art of justifying everything except intercourse.

"Just kissing."

"Just cuddling."

"Just sleeping in the same bed, but we didn't do anything."

"Just sending pictures."

"Just letting him touch me a little..."

Let's stop here.

Because while we're not technically having sex, we're definitely not pursuing holiness. Holiness isn't just about avoiding "big" sin. It's about setting yourself apart for God. It's about choosing obedience even when temptation whispers that "just a little" won't hurt.

The enemy isn't always trying to get you to fall off a cliff. Sometimes he just wants you to lean over the edge a little. That's how emotional bonds form. That's how clarity gets clouded. That's how your spirit grows numb to conviction. Not from leaping, but from leaning.

And here's the trap: blurred lines always bend toward compromise. When you live in the gray, you convince yourself that you're safe—but really, you're inching closer to the edge.

Intention is everything. Watching a movie and cuddling on the couch isn't sinful. But if the goal is to push the envelope, to see how far you can go without "going all the way," you've already lost the battle. Because testing your will in private is still disobedience in your heart. And when you put yourself in those situations, you *will* lose. The enemy knows it. That's why he keeps you playing with boundaries instead of fleeing from them.

This is where it gets real...we know what we're doing.

We know when we put on that outfit.

We know what time it is when we send that *"You up?"* text at midnight.

We know what it means when we invite him over.

This isn't about shame. It's about honesty. God isn't out to embarrass you. He wants to empower you. But empowerment starts with truth: the truth is that you can't flirt with fire and expect not to get burned.

And here's the good news. God doesn't leave you stuck in shame. He knows every boundary you've blurred, every "just a little" you've justified, and He still calls you His daughter. Conviction is proof of His love, not His rejection.

If you've crossed lines, it's not over for you. Purity isn't about your past, it's about your posture now. Holiness isn't about pretending you never fell, it's about surrendering so God can lift you back up.

But conviction is only the beginning. Awareness without action keeps you in the same cycle. Self-awareness is a gift, but it has to lead to change. God has already accounted for every mistake you'd ever make, but His grace isn't meant to keep you comfortable in sin. It's meant to empower you to walk free from it.

So instead of hiding, start healing. Instead of excuses, choose honesty. Instead of carrying weight alone, invite God—and trusted community—into the process. Conviction wakes you up, but obedience moves you forward.

Break the Cycle Before It Breaks You

Conviction is the wake-up call, but change requires a plan. Self-awareness without action keeps you stuck in the same loop: crying, confessing, and going right back to the place you fell. If you want freedom, you need both God's power and a strategy for your choices.

Breaking the cycle isn't about being stronger. It's about being wiser. It's about admitting where you're weak and setting up guardrails so you don't keep walking into the same trap.

Here are some practical ways to start:

- **Name your triggers.** You can't fight what you won't face. Is it the loneliness that hits late at night? That certain playlist that stirs up old memories? The "innocent" text that always leads somewhere it shouldn't? Write them down. Patterns lose their power when you drag them into the light.
- **Set boundaries that matter.** Boundaries aren't legalism, they're protection. If late-night hangouts keep leading to compromise, change the time. If movies at his place keep ending in blurred lines, change the location. Boundaries aren't about

restriction; they're about creating a space where holiness can breathe.

- **Invite accountability.** Freedom thrives in light. Find a trusted friend, mentor, or leader who can ask you hard questions without flinching. Isolation keeps cycles alive; honesty starves them. Accountability isn't weakness, it's wisdom.

- **Fast and pray.** Sometimes the cycle isn't just about behavior: it's about bondage. Your flesh has been fed more than your spirit. Fasting flips the script. It trains your heart to hunger for God more than the temporary comfort of compromise. Pair it with prayer and watch clarity return where confusion once lived.

- **Seek healing, not just control.** You can't grit your teeth through temptation and call it freedom. If the cycle is tied to rejection, abandonment, or past abuse, you need more than willpower: you need healing. Therapy, deliverance, prayer, journaling...don't be afraid to use every tool God provides. Control manages symptoms. Healing uproots the cause. Freedom is power plus a plan.

All Instead of "Almost"

You are not your past, and you are not your patterns. You are God's daughter, called to walk in wholeness, not "almost." When you choose His way, you don't just leave compromise behind. You step into clarity, peace, and strength you didn't know you had.

In the next chapter, you'll meet Derek and Brielle, a story that shows what happens when compromise goes unchecked. Their journey is a cautionary tale, but it's also a reminder: you don't have to live that story. God has already written something better for you. Their story will show the cost of "almost" and the grace God offers when we finally surrender.

...

Reflection

Before you turn the page, take time with these questions. Let them guide you past "almost" and into the wholeness God is calling you to.

1. *Where have you been living in "almost" — almost committed, almost obedient, almost surrendered — and how has it affected your walk with God?*
2. *How have cultural or church narratives (like counterfeits or kingdom spouse prophecies) shaped the way you view relationships, and what does God's Word say about them?*
3. *What boundaries or patterns do you need to surrender so you can break cycles instead of repeating them? What single boundary can I set this week that protects holiness instead of testing it?*

9| From Compromise to Chaos:

Derek & Brielle's Story

Brielle wasn't looking for drama. She was looking for a husband. After years of failed talking stages, awkward first dates, and watching friends walk down the aisle while she sat in the pew, she was tired of almost-love. She wanted covenant: real covering, real commitment.

She first noticed Derek at Bible study. He wasn't flashy, but he had a quiet confidence that drew people in. He knew Scripture well enough to hold his own discussion, but he also cracked jokes that made the room feel lighter. One day after class, he introduced himself and they began small talk. He asked if she wanted to grab coffee sometime to keep the conversation going. It wasn't a line: it felt genuine.

From there, Derek showed up in little ways that impressed her. He followed through on calls. He asked about her goals and listened like he cared about the answers. He prayed before meals, talked about wanting a family, and volunteered at church on weekends. He was not afraid to talk about a future with her. Compared to the half-hearted men she had dealt with, Derek seemed like a miracle wrapped in an amazing smile. For the first time in a long time, Brielle let herself believe she might be in the beginning of her answered prayer. And when your heart is that hopeful, it's easy to overlook the little things.

Behind the answered-prayer glow, Brielle noticed moments that didn't quite sit right: the way Derek dodged questions about his past, or how his prayer life seemed strong in public but thinner in private. He was always available for her, but rarely consistent with his own walk. Brielle noticed, but she quieted the questions. After all, hadn't she prayed for a man who loved God and pursued her?

Brielle found herself exhaling around him, telling herself, *Maybe this is it. Maybe the wait is finally over.* He wasn't perfect, but he looked close enough to what she had been asking God for that she didn't want to question it.

What she couldn't see was how quickly "close enough" would unravel into compromise, and how that compromise would eventually birth chaos.

The Shift:
From Boundaries to Blurred Lines

At first, Brielle and Derek tried to set the tone for their relationship with prayer and boundaries. They promised each other they wouldn't rush. They said the right words: *"Let's honor God with this."* And for a while, they believed it.

But slowly, their guard slipped. Prayer before dates got shorter. Conversations about faith faded into late-night talks on the couch. One kiss turned into many. "Just a little longer" became their excuse to stay wrapped up in each other's arms past midnight.

Brielle told herself they weren't doing anything "too serious." They hadn't had sex, so technically, they were fine. But the lines kept moving. Cuddling blurred into caressing. Boundaries blurred into loopholes. What they once called conviction now felt like "overthinking."

Deep down, Brielle felt it—that quiet nudge of the Holy Spirit—the heaviness in her chest after leaving Derek's apartment. But she silenced it with rationalization. *We're grown. We love each other. Marriage is coming anyway.* Derek reassured her too: *If God didn't want this, why would He bring us together?*

On Sundays, they looked like the model couple: hands raised in worship, sitting side by side in church. But Brielle noticed the shift: her prayers grew shorter, her Bible stayed closed longer. She didn't feel close to God anymore, but she felt close to Derek. And at the time, that felt like enough.

Have you ever confused emotional closeness with spiritual connection?

Her boundaries hadn't shattered in one night: they eroded, inch by inch, until compromise looked like connection. What seemed like love was really the slow drift of her heart away from obedience.

The Slide:
When the Love Nest Becomes a Cage

The shift from boundaries to blurry lines set the stage for something bigger. When Derek's lease ended, the conversation about living together slipped in almost casually. "I don't want to move back in with my parents," he said one night, scrolling through his phone. "And rent's crazy right now. Honestly, it just makes sense for us to combine resources. Why waste money on two places when we're headed toward marriage anyway?"

Brielle froze for a moment. She had heard sermons against cohabitation. Her parents had even made negative comments about "shacking up." But she also felt the pull of practicality...and the fear of losing what they had built.

We love each other. We're serious. Engagement is coming soon, she told herself. *Besides, we'll set boundaries. We can make this work.*

One weekend, Derek carried his boxes into her apartment. They dressed it up as wisdom, calling it "preparing for marriage." To everyone else, it looked like progress. To Brielle, it felt like security: no more nights alone, no more wondering where things were headed.

But the spiritual weight was immediate. Their prayer life, already shrinking, nearly disappeared. Disagreements that used to resolve in hours stretched into days. Derek became comfortable, even complacent. He had the benefits of covenant without the cost of commitment. What was once pursuit became convenience, and convenience can't sustain covenant.

He saw marriage as a distant future goal. And Brielle, though she wouldn't admit it out loud, began to feel the ache of disobedience in her spirit.

She ignored it, clinging to the hope of a ring, convincing herself the tension was just "growing pains." But deep down, she knew something holy had been traded for something hollow.

What started as a love nest slowly became a cage...one compromise at a time.

The Fallout:
When Compromise Bears Fruit

The unraveling didn't happen in one big explosion. It was slow, like a thread pulled loose until the whole fabric came apart. Compromise rarely feels destructive at first. It feels comfortable: but comfort outside of obedience always costs more later.

At first, Brielle convinced herself the tension was normal. All couples argue. All relationships go through rough patches. But the cracks widened. What started as playful debates turned into sharp words. Nights once filled with laughter turned into silent scrolling on opposite ends of the couch.

Derek grew less attentive and hyper-focused on his career goals. He stopped making plans. He brushed off her questions about marriage with vague promises: *"Soon. We'll get there. I just need a little more time."* Brielle clung to those words like lifelines, but deep down, they felt empty.

Meanwhile, her spirit was unraveling. She still showed up at church, still raised her hands in worship, but inside she felt broken. She prayed less and apologized more...as if God needed convincing to take her back each time she crossed another boundary. Her journal pages filled with questions: *Why do I feel so far from You, Lord? Why do I feel trapped?*

She had given Derek covenant-level access without covenant covering, and the cost was catching up to her. Her peace eroded. Her confidence fractured. Even her sense of identity felt fragile. Who was she apart from Derek now?

And this is where compromise shows its fruit: what felt like peace now felt like pressure.

The final thread snapped when Derek finally admitted he wasn't ready for marriage, and maybe never would be. Brielle's world collapsed. She wasn't just heartbroken. She was humiliated. She had defended him to friends, silenced her own convictions, and invested years of her life in a man who had no intention of being her lifelong partner.

The breakup left her with more than pain. It left her with regret. Regret for ignoring God's nudges. Regret for calling compromise wisdom. Regret for mistaking convenience for covenant.

She took her hurt feelings to God, embarrassed at first, but over time she began to feel Him putting her heart back together. She promised herself that next time, she would listen to Him.

The Mirror: Why This Story Matters

Sis, Derek and Brielle aren't just characters on a page—they're a mirror. A mirror that shows us that collapse doesn't begin with a blowout. It begins with small choices that look harmless in the moment but carry heavy consequences over time.

Maybe you've had a Derek: someone who looked like an answered prayer but left you drained. Maybe you've been a Brielle: brushing aside conviction because you didn't want to lose what felt like love. Or maybe you're in that in-between space now, hoping the cracks you see will fix themselves if you just hold on long enough.

This isn't about pointing fingers at men or piling shame on women. It's about seeing patterns for what they are. Half-commitments don't build wholeness. They build confusion. They leave you wrestling with situations God never intended for you to be in.

The good news is you don't have to stay there. God doesn't show us ourselves in stories like Derek and Brielle's to condemn us. He shows us so we can wake up. So, we can see where compromise leads and decide, *not me, not anymore.*

Their story ends in collapse, but that isn't the only story. God gives us wisdom for a better way, and His Word is a blueprint for building with clarity instead of chaos.

In the next chapter, we'll unpack that blueprint together. And then we'll meet Maya and Elijah, a couple whose journey shows us what it looks like when alignment takes the lead.

10| From Conviction to Clarity:

Derek and Brielle's story showed us how easy it is to go from good intentions to compromise, and how costly that slide can become. But God doesn't just give warnings; He gives guidance. He doesn't just tell us what to avoid. He shows us how to build something better.

Sis, I don't want you to only hear principles in passing. I want you to have a blueprint you can come back to emotions get loud and boundaries feel blurry. Bookmark this. Screenshot it. Write it down if you need to. Here's my gift to you: The 10-Step Christian Dating Blueprint.

The 10-Step
Christian Dating Blueprint
When You've Met Someone Worth Exploring

1. Start With Surrender
Scripture: Proverbs 3:5-6
*"Trust in the Lord with all your heart and
lean not on your own understanding;
in all your ways submit to him,
and he will make your paths straight."*

Remember: Dating is not a shortcut to wholeness or a reward for good behavior. It's a space that God wants to guide, just like every other area of your life.

Your Mindset: "God, I want your best for me more than I want to be chosen."

His Mindset: He's also surrendered. He's not idolizing marriage or using you to fill a void. He's seeking God and allowing Him to lead.

Practical Application: Before you even say yes to that first date, ask: Have I invited God into this? Am I letting Him shape my desires, not just co-sign them?

2. Date With Clarity
Scripture: 1 Corinthians 14:33

"For God is not a God of confusion but of peace."

Remember: Confusion isn't always a feeling. It shows up in patterns, mixed signals, and inconsistency. And remember: peace isn't the same as permission. God also speaks through conviction, correction, and even discomfort.

Your Mindset: "Clarity is kindness, not pressure. I deserve to know where this is going."

His Mindset: He communicates with intention. He's clear, consistent, and emotionally available. Not leading with charm but with character.

Practical Application: Pay attention to both your feelings and the facts. Is he honoring your boundaries? Is there alignment between his words and his actions? Do your own words and actions align?

3. Know the Assignment

Scripture: Amos 3:3

"Can two walk together unless they are agreed?"

Remember: You are not just dating for vibes or chemistry alone; a husband is a purpose partner.

Your Mindset: "I know who I am and where I'm going. I need someone who's not just a believer, but a builder."

His Mindset: He's not intimidated by your calling. He's walking in his own assignment and looking for a teammate, not a fan.

Practical Application: Share your God-given vision and goals early. Ask him about his. Does your connection sharpen your purpose or distract from it?

4. Talk Real, Talk Early

Scripture: Proverbs 20:5

"The purposes of a person's heart are deep waters, but one who has insight draws them out."

Remember: You can't discover compatibility without conversation. Depth doesn't just happen, it's pursued.

Your Mindset: "If I'm afraid to ask real questions, I might be more focused on keeping him rather than truly knowing him."

His Mindset: He's not surface-level. He asks intentional questions and gives thoughtful answers. He's not dodging emotional depth or spiritual topics.

Practical Application: Ask about his relationship with God, past relationships, future goals, and emotional/mental health. Don't assume alignment, confirm it.

5. Protect the Pace

Scripture: Song of Songs 2:7

"Do not arouse or awaken love until it so desires."

Remember: Love grows over time, but God's timing doesn't always look like a clock. What matters isn't speed; it's alignment.

Your Mindset: "I'm not in a rush to secure a title. I'm learning if this connection can carry covenant. Whether it's six months or six years, I want God to be the one setting the pace."

His Mindset: He's patient, not pushy. He honors your boundaries and has his own. He discerns timing with wisdom, not urgency. He isn't driven by the fear of missing out, but by the desire to walk in God's will.

Practical Application: Don't measure your journey by someone else's timeline. Ask God, "What pace honors You in this connection?" Ask yourself: "Is our pace protecting purpose or feeding pressure?" Keep checking in with your spirit, not your social media feed.

6. Watch the Fruit

Scripture: Matthew 7:16

"By their fruit you will recognize them."

Remember: A man can say the right things and still not live them. And you can intend to do the right things, and still miss the mark. Fruit takes time.

Your Mindset: "I don't need perfect, but I need consistent. I'd rather wait for fruit than fall for flash. I also want to display the same fruit that I desire to see in my partner."

His Mindset: He doesn't just talk about faith, he lives it. He's accountable, humble, and open to growth.

Practical Application: Be spiritually consistent and look for the same. Pay attention to how he treats others, how he handles conflict, and whether his values match his habits.

7. Listen to Wise Counsel
Scripture: Proverbs 11:14

"Where there is no guidance, a people falls, but in an abundance of counselors there is safety."

Remember: God often confirms through wise, trusted voices, not just our own feelings.

Your Mindset: "God didn't design me to date in isolation. The people who know me well can help me see what I miss."

His Mindset: He's open to input from spiritually mature people in your life. He doesn't get defensive when others lovingly challenge him or ask deeper questions.

Practical Application: Let mentors, Godly friends, and spiritual leaders speak into the relationship. Don't hide the connection from your community if you claim it's from God.

8. Watch How He Leads... and How You Follow

Scripture: Luke 16:10

"Whoever is faithful with very little will also be faithful with much..."

Remember: Dating is not the time to play house or test submission. It's the time to observe responsibility and your response.

Your Mindset: "I'm not looking for a perfect leader, but I am watching how he leads himself. Am I showing up as the woman God called me to be, or am I shrinking or controlling?"

His Mindset: He's not just a talker. He takes initiative, honors his word, and makes decisions with prayer and wisdom. He isn't passive or pushy. He's intentional.

Practical Application: Pay attention to whether he leads in love, communication, and spiritual matters. And check how you respond. Are you controlling everything out of fear, or trusting God enough to let a man lead?

9. Don't Confuse Peace with Perfection

Scripture: Philippians 4:7

"And the peace of God, which surpasses all understanding, will guard your hearts and your minds in Christ Jesus."

Remember: God's peace isn't the absence of emotion — it's the presence of clarity, even when vulnerability is real.

Your Mindset: "I'm not chasing a perfect situation. I'm looking for alignment with God, even if that includes tension that stretches me."

His Mindset: He doesn't just make you *feel good*; he brings stability to your spirit. He isn't inconsistent or sending mixed signals. He contributes to peace, not confusion.

Practical Application: Don't confuse butterflies for God's peace. Pay attention to whether your spirit feels guarded and steady when you're with him or shaken up by uncertainty.

10. Pray Through, Not Just About It
Scripture: James 1:5

"If any of you lacks wisdom, you should ask God, who gives generously to all without finding fault,
and it will be given to you."

Remember: Prayer isn't just a checkbox. It's dialogue that helps you discern clearly.

Your Mindset: "I'm not just praying about him, I'm praying through every step with God, staying submitted and surrendered."

His Mindset: He initiates prayer, participates in spiritual growth, and doesn't rely on your faith to carry the relationship. He desires to grow *with* you in Christ.

Practical Application: Pray together and individually—not to force a yes from God but to remain open to whatever He says.

Principles are powerful, but they hit different when you see them lived out. That's where Maya and Elijah come in: not as a perfect couple, but as a real picture of what happens when two people put this blueprint into practice.

Maya & Elijah's Story

Maya wanted marriage, and she wasn't ashamed of it. She didn't bury the desire or pretend it didn't matter. She was straight with God about it: the loneliness, the longing to be chosen, the dream of building a life with someone who loved Him too.

But here's what changed. God started pressing her to ask *why*. Why did she want to be a wife? Was it status? Security? The fairytale ending she thought would fix everything? Through prayer, journaling, and quiet conviction, God showed her that wanting marriage wasn't wrong. Idolizing it was. He reshaped her desire and taught her what surrendering it looked like. It didn't mean burying it; it meant trusting Him enough to let Him refine it.

So, when Elijah showed up at a friend's game night—no angels singing, no prophetic dream, just laughter over a heated round of Uno—Maya met him from a different posture. She wasn't grasping for validation or secretly testing him against a mental checklist. She was simply being her God-authentic self.

Elijah noticed it right away. Her confidence. Her peace. The way she was fully present without trying to prove herself. By the end of the night, he asked for her number. And instead of spiraling into *"Is he the one?"* Maya just said yes. Not from desperation, but from the kind of surrender that trusts God to lead the story instead of forcing it.

No Guessing Games

From the beginning, Elijah didn't leave Maya guessing. After their first meet-up, he didn't disappear for days or send vague late-night "Wyd" texts. He called when he said he would. He asked intentional questions. And when he wanted to see her again, he made it clear.

For Maya, that was new. She was used to mixed signals: men who said all the right things but kept her in the fog. *We'll see where this goes. I'm not ready for labels, but I think you're cool.* That type of back-and-forth had left her drained in the past.

Elijah was different. His intentionality wasn't just personality: it flowed from his walk with God. He was upfront about his faith, about how his relationship with Christ shaped his decisions, and about his desire to honor God in how he pursued her. He didn't overpromise, but he also didn't keep her in the dark.

Maya realized clarity wasn't about rushing toward marriage on the second date: it was about consistency.

Words and actions that lined up. Intentions that weren't buried under charm.

And because Maya continued to surrender her desire, she didn't confuse peace with passivity. She paid attention. She matched Elijah's clear intentions with her own. She didn't shrink back or wait for him to read her mind. She asked her own questions. She spoke honestly about her goals, her boundaries, her faith.

There were no games to play. Just two people walking in the light and letting that light reveal whether they had a foundation worth building on.

Purpose Over Vibes

By their third or fourth time hanging out, Maya and Elijah were already talking about purpose. Not in an interview style, but in real conversations that revealed where their lives were headed. And it went beyond career goals or the "where do you see yourself in 10 years" small talk. They were asking each other bigger questions: *What do you believe God has called you to do on this earth? In what capacity are you supposed to serve Him?*

Maya told Elijah about her vision. She wanted to help women entrepreneurs—especially in marketing—build businesses with integrity, not manipulation. She wanted her work to be excellent, but also honest. And she didn't want to hide her faith to do it. For her, purpose wasn't limited to a church pew. It was about being light in spaces that didn't always welcome it.

Elijah shared his own calling: pouring into teenage boys who grew up without fathers. He'd been mentoring in his community, and for him, purpose looked like showing up, being present, and helping his mentees avoid the same traps he had seen take down too many young men.

Neither of their callings required a pulpit, but both carried the fingerprints of God. They were showing up authentically in the spaces He had placed them, using their gifts to impact the world around them.

As the conversation kept flowing, it naturally shifted into how their purposes might align down the road. Nothing heavy or pressured: just lighthearted what-ifs about serving side by side, about how two people could cover more ground together than apart. Elijah wasn't afraid to mention the future, even though they were still in the talking stage. For Maya, that was refreshing. Too many men she'd met dodged the future altogether, as if bringing it up too soon meant signing a contract.

But Elijah made it clear without making it intense. He didn't want a fan; he wanted a partner. He wanted a woman living out her own God-given assignment, one that could complement and strengthen his.

For Maya, that was enough to keep leaning into the friendship, to keep testing and approving whether this connection was in step with God's will (Romans 12:2). Conversations like this didn't seal the deal, but they did reveal potential worth exploring: two people walking in the same direction, willing to ask *"Can we build something together that honors Him?"*

Hard Questions, Honest Answers

Maya had been down the road of surface-level before, and it always left her disappointed. She was used to men who could talk for hours about music, work, and sports, but shut down the second she asked anything deeper. Elijah wasn't like that.

Early on, Maya decided she wasn't going to tiptoe around the hard stuff. She asked him about past relationships, about how he handled conflict, about what he learned from his mistakes. She asked where he struggled, what he was praying about, and how he saw himself growing in the future.

To her surprise, Elijah didn't dodge. He didn't get defensive or try to flip the questions back on her to deflect. He answered. Honestly. Sometimes awkwardly. Sometimes with a pause while he thought about it. But he answered. And he asked her the same.

It wasn't an interrogation. Just conversation that flowed naturally. And it felt different because it was mutual. Elijah wanted to know her heart as much as she wanted to know his.

For Maya, that honesty was refreshing. Not because Elijah gave perfect answers, but because he gave real ones. He didn't pretend to be stronger than he was. He didn't put on a polished church-boy front. And that let Maya drop her guard too.

This was the kind of transparency that built trust. Not guarantees. Not fairy tales. This was a recipe for a steady foundation that could hold weight if the relationship kept moving forward.

Slow Enough to Last

Things with Elijah didn't feel rushed. He wasn't blowing up Maya's phone all day or trying to spend every waking hour together. He pursued her, yes, but with balance. Some nights were dinner and long talks, and some nights were spent focusing on their individual lives. That rhythm gave their connection space to breathe instead of burning out.

In the past, Maya had mistaken speed for seriousness. If a man texted non-stop or wanted to see her every day, she read it as commitment. But usually it was just intensity, a fire that flared hot and fizzled just as fast. But things were moving differently with Elijah. He wasn't in a hurry to slap a title on what they had. He was willing to build slowly, letting trust grow as naturally as attraction. That pace felt new for Maya, and if she was honest, it gave her some anxiety. She wasn't used to a connection that didn't demand constant contact.

But even without daily blow-ups of her phone, Elijah was steady. He checked in. A quick text, a thoughtful voice note, a moment that let her know she was on his mind. He didn't flood her with words, but his consistency spoke louder.

Protecting the pace didn't mean dragging their feet or keeping things casual forever. It meant moving in step with God instead of rushing ahead. It meant asking, *"Is this growing in a way that honors Him?"* instead of *"How fast can we get to the next milestone?"*

Slow wasn't boring. Slow was steady. And steady was what Maya realized could last.

Patterns Over Promises

As Maya spent more time with Elijah, she started to feel more grounded. Not because everything was perfect, but because his patterns spoke louder than his promises. He was the same man on Thursday night after Bible study as he was on a random Tuesday after work. Thoughtful. Steady. Honest about his shortcomings.

When Maya mentioned her car needing an oil change, Elijah remembered and reminded her about it days later. His consistent attention to detail wasn't loud or flashy, but it was fruit. Not the kind that shows up on a first date when everybody is on their best behavior, but the kind that grows slowly over time.

Maya had learned the hard way that charm fades and charisma can mask chaos. But fruit? That's what lasts. And even fruit gets tested.

One night after a long day at work, Elijah was short with Maya on the phone. She was already feeling sensitive after a hard day at work herself, and his tone hit her wrong. Instead of being honest about the offense, she pulled back. The next day, she didn't return his texts. She didn't feel like pretending nothing had happened.

Elijah noticed the shift and called. Not to argue, but to ask, "Did I do something to upset you?"

Maya hesitated, then admitted, "Yeah...I felt like you were being short with me, and I just....shut down."

Elijah listened without defensiveness. "I apologize. I didn't mean to make you feel that way. I was worn out, but I should've said that instead of snapping."

Maya apologized for ghosting, and they quickly moved on, laughing about the misunderstanding.

That moment could've turned messy; instead, humility reset the tone. In the past, Maya might've let distance harden into silence, and Elijah might've ignored the tension until it faded. But this time, they leaned in.

It wasn't about chemistry anymore. It was about character. About humility.

That conversation, awkward and vulnerable as it was, meant more to Maya than any compliment ever could. Elijah didn't just know scripture; he lived it. And Maya was learning how to speak the truth without shutting down.

Their peace didn't come from sweeping issues under the rug. It came from letting fruit speak louder than feelings.

Don't Date in the Dark

Maya and Elijah didn't treat their connection like a secret. From the beginning, they invited trusted voices into the process.

Maya talked with her closest friends who knew her patterns, prayed with her, and weren't afraid to challenge her if they saw red flags. She didn't just give them a highlight reel; she told them her real feelings. When she mentioned Elijah to her mentor, the first thing her mentor asked was, *"So how's your spirit when you're around him? More distracted or more anchored?"* That question alone kept Maya honest.

Elijah wasn't closed off either. He had men in his life who held him accountable, who knew his tendencies and could call him out if they saw him drifting. When Elijah told them about Maya, they didn't just hype him up. They asked about his intentions. They reminded him, *"Don't play with her heart. Be clear about where you want things to go."*

But wise counsel didn't always sound easy. One of Maya's friends noticed her patterns and said it plainly: *"You like him, but you're guarded. You pull back the moment things feel too real. If you don't let your walls down, you'll sabotage this before you even know what God wants to do."*

Maya tensed. Her first instinct was to defend herself. *"You just don't get it."* The comment stung because it exposed something she hadn't wanted to admit: she was terrified that the moment she opened her heart fully, Elijah would hurt her like the others had.

That night, instead of dismissing it, she prayed. She journaled. And the Spirit confirmed what her friend said: love can't grow where fear runs the show. Vulnerability wasn't about being reckless; it was about trusting God enough to take the risk, knowing that He will come to the rescue, no matter what.

This new perspective didn't magically erase her fears, but it did shift her posture. It reminded her that guarding her heart doesn't mean locking it away. It means giving it to God while still being open to love.

Elijah faced his own test. When he admitted to this mentor that sometimes he wrestled with sexual temptation, his friend didn't let him off the hook. *"Then build guardrails before you wreck yourself,"* he said flatly. It stung, but it reminded Elijah that pursuing Maya wasn't just about good intentions, but accountability.

For Maya and Elijah, these moments proved that community didn't weaken their connection. It made it stronger. Counsel didn't make the decisions for them. But it gave them clarity. It gave them accountability. And it reminded them both that a relationship rooted in God doesn't grow in the dark.

More Than Words

Maya knew leadership wasn't about titles or who picked the restaurant. It was about how Elijah handled responsibility when things weren't easy. And the truth? It wasn't always easy.

There was one night when the attraction between them ran strong, and the temptation whispered louder than conviction. They'd been on the couch talking, laughing, leaning in closer than they meant to. The air shifted. One more touch and the line would've been blurred.

They both noticed it. Instead of pretending it wasn't happening, Elijah shifted the moment. "I think I need to head out," he said gently, standing before it went any further. It felt abrupt, almost awkward, but it was intentional. He wasn't running from Maya. He was protecting both of them.

The next time they hung out, Elijah brought it up. Not in a heavy-handed way, but with quiet conviction. "We should probably set some boundaries," he said. "I don't want to risk putting us in the wrong spot again. So, maybe no late nights, less time with just us at home, and more public or group things. I want to protect this, and you."

For Maya, it was awkward at first. No man she'd dated had ever suggested something like that. Part of her thought, *Is this childish? Do we really need rules like this?* But the longer she sat with it, the more she realized what was really happening. Elijah wasn't just protecting himself. He was leading her. Protecting their budding relationship. And most of all, protecting their walk with God.

And then there were disagreements. No relationship moves forward without them, and theirs was no exception.

In the past, Maya could go days without speaking after a conflict, shutting down until the other person chased her.

Elijah caught on to that early. So, when tension showed up between them, he didn't pressure her, but he didn't ignore it either.

The next day, he texted: *I know you may need a couple days, but I don't like how we left things yesterday. I'd like to talk soon.*

That softened her. Instead of dragging it out for days, Maya responded quicker than she would have before, and they were able to work through it together.

It wasn't always neat or easy. Sometimes they still circled the same issue two or three times before landing on understanding. But the difference was in how they handled it. Elijah leaned in instead of withdrawing. Maya opened up instead of shutting down. And slowly, they were building a new pattern: one where conflict didn't create distance but became a place to practice honesty, humility, and grace.

It turned out leadership wasn't loud or glamorous. It was the quiet stuff, like ending the night early, starting hard conversations, admitting when you're wrong. And following wasn't weakness. It was trust, honesty, and courage to stay soft when shutting down felt easier. That's what set Maya and Elijah apart: they weren't chasing perfect moments. They were practicing Godly ones.

Calm in the Chaos

Just as Maya and Elijah were finding their rhythm, peace got tested. One late-night call changed everything. Elijah's younger brother had been in a serious car wreck, and the fallout shook not just his world, but their relationship too.

Elijah dropped everything to be there for his family. Hospital visits, late nights, financial worries—it all landed on his shoulders. For the first time since they met, he wasn't as present with Maya. His texts got shorter, his calls less frequent, his mind clearly somewhere else.

Maya felt it. The old version would've taken the distance personally. *He's pulling away. Maybe he's not serious. Maybe he doesn't want me after all.* The insecurity whispered louder than truth. But she also knew this wasn't about her. It was about real life. And real life had a way of exposing whether a relationship was built on fantasy or faith.

Still, miscommunication crept in. Elijah assumed Maya understood his silence. Maya assumed his silence meant disinterest. It was a clash of expectations that could've unraveled everything.

Instead of ghosting or letting the distance grow, Maya prayed. She had prayed about their relationship before, but this time felt different...heavier. Desperate, even. She poured out her heart, asking God not just to fix the tension but to show her how to respond. And for the first time, she realized prayer wasn't only about unloading her feelings; it was about listening long enough to let Him guide her next step.

When Maya finally reached out to Elijah one evening, they ended up on the phone. She asked how he was holding up, hoping this time he might open up more. Elijah's voice was heavy, worn. His answers stayed vague: "I'm fine...just tired...been at the hospital most of the day."

Maya hesitated, then chose her words carefully. "Well, I don't want to press, but I am really concerned about you...and I guess I feel a little shut out."

Elijah let out a long sigh. "My intention isn't to shut you out. I do want you to be here. I just don't know how to balance everything right now."

Before she could respond, his tone shifted. "Hey, my mom's calling me. I've got to go. We'll talk soon, ok?"

Maya quickly said "Ok," and the line went quiet. His words gave Maya a flicker of hope, but it wasn't enough to steady her. If anything, she hung up feeling the weight of uncertainty more than before.

But as the silence settled, so did something else. In the very place in her heart where she and Elijah felt shaky, God felt steady. Maya couldn't predict if this would end in love or heartbreak, but she knew she wasn't left guessing about God. His presence wrapped around her like an anchor in the storm, reminding her that even if Elijah couldn't carry her right now, her Father could.

For the first time, she saw what peace really meant. It wasn't a perfect relationship or having all the answers. It was knowing God was still there, unshaken, even when everything else felt fragile.

When Prayer Becomes the Process

After that phone call, Maya sat in the quiet, replaying every word. Elijah wasn't gone, but he wasn't really present either. She wanted to press him harder, but the Holy Spirit nudged her: *be present, not pushy.*

So, she showed up quietly. A text here. A call there. Nothing heavy, nothing demanding. She let him know she was praying with him, but she saved her deepest wrestling for God. And in those prayers, her posture changed. She still wanted Elijah, but she wanted God's will more. Prayer stopped being a reaction to her emotions and became a process that shaped her responses.

As much as she fought the urge to pull back, she leaned into presence. And when she heard Elijah's brother was headed into surgery, she asked if she could meet him at the hospital. He agreed.

That night, something shifted. They prayed together before the surgery—holding hands, voices trembling, but anchored by God. They had prayed together before, but this was different. It wasn't about asking for a good date or for clarity about their feelings. It was about standing before God as two people who were learning how to carry weight together.

When Elijah's brother made it through surgery and began to recover, the relief on Elijah's face was unmistakable. And so was his gratitude. One evening not long after, he finally opened up to Maya:

"I need you to know how much I appreciate you. You didn't walk away when I shut down. You stayed. That showed me something I can't ignore. I don't just want to date you. I want to do life with you. My prayer is that one day we'll be husband and wife, because you've proven you're a true partner."

Maya's eyes filled with tears. She told him the truth: "Your consistency pushed me to show up in ways I was afraid to before. I've been softened and stretched in the best ways because of how you lead with character."

That conversation didn't end in a ring, but it did seal a new level of commitment. They weren't perfect. They had struggled, stumbled, and questioned. But their foundation wasn't vibes or fairytales. It was prayer, presence, and practical choices to keep God in the middle.

Fast forward...

Over the next year, Maya and Elijah's relationship was anything but flawless. There were still moments of miscommunication, differences in how they handled stress, and plenty of learning curves. But instead of letting those moments drive them apart, they leaned into the same rhythm that had carried them through before: honesty, prayer, and a willingness to grow.

Every high and low stretched them: not just as individuals, but as a couple. Elijah learned to share his weight instead of carrying it alone. Maya learned to stay soft and present instead of shutting down when things felt tense.

And together, they discovered that Godly love was never about avoiding struggle. It was about walking through it hand in hand, with Him in the middle.

So, when Elijah proposed, it didn't feel rushed or uncertain. It felt like the next step in a journey God had already been shaping. By then, they both knew marriage would bring its own challenges and joy, but they also knew they were ready. Not because they had it all figured out, but because they were certain God was preparing them for covenant. They trusted that as long as they kept surrendering and seeking Him, He would continue to sanctify them...even after I do.

Foundation Over Fairytale

Maya and Elijah's story wasn't flawless, and that's exactly why it matters. They didn't stumble into covenant by accident or wing it on vibes. They walked through the blueprint step by step—surrender, clarity, boundaries, counsel, prayer—and those choices gave them something stronger than chemistry. They built a foundation.

Derek and Brielle, on the other hand, skipped the process. They leaned on feelings, blurred lines, and compromise, and when the weight of real life hit, their relationship collapsed. What looked promising in the beginning never had the structure to last.

That's the difference between chasing a fairytale and building on faith. Fairytales collapse under pressure. Foundations stand, even when the wind hits hard.

Sis, that's why the steps matter. Not because they guarantee you a husband, but because they anchor you in God. The blueprint doesn't just prepare you to choose well, it prepares you to become the kind of woman who can build something lasting when the right man does come along.

But here's the part we don't like to admit. Even with the right steps in place, your posture matters too. Maya's story wasn't carried by Elijah alone. Her softness, her honesty, her patience, and her willingness to let God lead made space for the relationship to grow.

Godly relationships don't just collapse because of poor leadership from men. They can also unravel when we, as women, step out of alignment with God's design. Without understanding biblical femininity, we risk sabotaging what God is building...even when He's given us the right man and the right foundation.

And that's where we're headed next.

...

Reflection

Before we move on, pause here. Maya and Elijah's story wasn't just a sweet ending: it was proof that the steps matter, and that your posture matters too. So, let's bring this closer to home.

1. *Which of the ten steps challenged you the most... and why?*

2. *When you think about your past relationships, do you see more of Derek and Brielle's patterns or Maya and Elijah's? What does that reveal about your foundation?*

3. *How can prayer become your process right now — not just a reaction, but a rhythm that shapes your choices?*

11| The Strength of Soft

Maya's story didn't begin at the altar. The real transformation started long before she said yes to Elijah, and long before she met him. It began when she said yes to God. Her story reminds us that a Godly relationship isn't built on charm, timing, or even chemistry. It's built on posture: the condition of the heart that decides whether you'll walk with God's grace or try to grind your way through life on your own.

And the reality is, posture is where many of us struggle. We've had to survive. We've learned to take care of ourselves, protect ourselves, and prove ourselves—all while carrying responsibilities we were never meant to shoulder alone. Somewhere along the way, strength became our shield. Independence became our identity. Control became our comfort.

But strength without surrender isn't peace. It's exhaustion dressed up as stability.

God never asked us to stop being strong. He asked us to learn how to be *soft in His hands*. To be women who know when to lead and when to lean. Women who can hold power and still carry peace.

Biblical femininity isn't about losing your edge. It's about learning how to use it with wisdom. It's the posture that says, "I can be capable and still need covering. I can be bold and still gentle. I can move with confidence because I'm led by the Spirit, not my scars."

So, before we talk about what femininity looks like in dating or marriage, we have to start with the posture of your heart. Because if your posture is off, everything else will be too.

What Biblical Femininity Isn't

Let's clear something up right away: to be feminine, according to the Bible, is not about pretending to be fragile or losing your voice to keep the peace. Somewhere along the way, "submissive," got confused with "silent," and "gentle" started sounding like "weak." That's not the woman God designed you to be.

You were made in His image; bold, discerning, and capable of carrying wisdom and strength at the same time. The Proverbs 31 woman wasn't a pushover. She ran businesses, managed her household, served her community, and still made space for kindness and reverence to shape her every move. Her power came from posture, not performance.

Being biblically feminine doesn't mean you stop leading where God called you to lead. It means you learn how to lead *from* the Spirit, not from striving. It means you stop proving your worth and start walking like you already know it.

And it's definitely not about dimming your light so a man can feel brighter next to you. The right man won't be intimidated by your glow. He'll see it as confirmation that you're walking with God.

Real femininity is rooted, not reactive. It's tender without being timid. It's confident without being controlling. It's the balance that can only come from knowing who you are and whose you are.

When Survival Turns Masculine

For a lot of us, "strong" was never a choice. It was survival. We became the fixers, the planners, the ones who made it happen because no one else would. And at first, that strength felt empowering...until it started to harden us.

When you've spent years protecting yourself, it's easy to start living like God needs your help too. You stop waiting on Him and start managing outcomes. You stop trusting people and start controlling everything that feels uncertain. What once was resilience quietly turns into resistance, not just toward men, but toward God.

That's what happens when survival turns masculine. You move from resting in God's covering to trying to become your own.

But here's the catch: you can't receive love with the same hands you use to fight. When your guard is always up, even the right man will feel like a threat instead of a gift. And when your heart is closed, even God's correction starts to sound like criticism.

Hear me, Sis. Your strength is not the problem. The problem begins when strength becomes your identity instead of a tool. God designed you to be powerful, but under His authority. To be decisive, but also discerning. To be capable, but still covered.

Softness isn't the opposite of strength. It's the evidence that you're safe enough to stop surviving and start resting.

"Soft Girl Era" vs. Spirit-Led Softness

Everywhere you look, softness is trending. "Soft girl season." "Soft life." "Feminine energy." Women are tired of hustling, striving, and being in fight mode. And honestly? That desire makes sense. We weren't created to live in constant self-protection.

But here's where it gets tricky: culture softness says, "make life easier," while spiritual softness says, "let God make you stronger."

One version invites escape. The other invites transformation.

The "soft girl era" tells you to pamper yourself, keep your nails done, light a candle, or protect your peace. But peace isn't something you protect. It's something you *possess* when your life is surrendered to God.

There's nothing wrong with wanting rest or beauty. But biblical femininity doesn't stop at aesthetics. True softness is the posture of a women who's submitted, not just styled: who's calm because her confidence is in Christ, not her circumstances.

Scripture calls it a "gentle and quiet spirit" (1 Peter 3:4). That doesn't mean muted. It means anchored. It's the kind of peace that can sit in a storm without performing for approval. The kind that knows when to speak and when to stay silent, because both can be power when led by the Spirit.

Softness isn't weakness or self-reliance. It's wisdom wrapped in grace. The world markets it. God matures it.

Let Him Lead, Sis

Some of us could run a small country with how well we organize our lives. And it shows up in how we portray ourselves in the dating world. Some of us plan the date, set the tone, define the relationship, and still send a thank-you text after. Not because we're desperate, but because we've been trained to make things happen. We're efficient, capable go-getters.

But if we're not careful, control can slowly creep in. We say, "I'm just being intentional," when what we really mean is, "I don't trust anyone else to handle it."

That's not leadership. That's management.

Letting him lead doesn't mean you stop showing up or speaking up. It means you stop trying to steer what God is already guiding. It's about trust. It's giving space for leadership to grow while still being fully engaged: prayerful, observant, and wise.

A Godly woman doesn't follow blindly. She follows with sound judgment. She watches for fruit, not just feelings. She sees if his words align with his walk, if his prayer life matches his plans, and if his humility leaves room for God to correct him.

And when she sees that kind of fruit, she leads in her femininity with wisdom, grace, and peace that invite partnership instead of power struggles. She doesn't just look for a man that lives like Jesus. She strives to do the same.

This is how she leads *while* letting him lead:
She communicates needs with clarity, not control.
She expresses opinions with humility, not hostility.
She challenges with respect, not resentment.
She builds, she encourages, and she prays: not to change him, but to cover him.

That's feminine strength. It doesn't demand attention. It draws it.

When a woman walks in peace, she creates an environment where a man can lead without fear of competition. And when a man leads through Christ, he creates a space where she can rest without losing her voice. That's what mutual submission looks like —not one shrinking, not one dominating, but both surrendered to the same God.

So, maybe the issue isn't that we're holding too tightly to the pen of our lives. Maybe it's that we've forgotten the posture.

Letting a man lead starts with letting God lead *you*. Because if you can't trust His covering, you'll always compete with the one He sends to reflect it.

The right kind of leadership thrives where peace lives, and peace starts with you. The way you listen. The way you respond. The way you release control and still stay present.

That's how Godly partnership grows: when both people know their strength and still choose to surrender.

And that's where the balance begins.

The Beauty of Balance

Balance is where femininity turns from theory into transformation. It's not about pretending to be perfect. It's about learning how to respond with peace when life tests your posture.

Real life *will* test your softness. Some men will lead with integrity. Others will lead with ego. But a Godly woman doesn't mirror behavior, she models Christ. Her strength shows up in restraint, not retaliation.

Here's what that looks like in everyday moments when getting to know someone:

When he plans the date but doesn't follow through: Give him space to lead, but don't excuse inconsistency. A Godly woman practices grace, but she also honors her own time. A response could look like, "Hey, I noticed our plans didn't happen. I value consistency, so I'm going to step back from this. I wish you the best." It sets a standard without shaming. It communicates peace and accountability at the same time.

When conversation turns into competition:

You don't have to match tone to prove your point. Stay grounded. Respond with calm confidence. *"I don't want to argue. I'd rather understand where you're coming from."* It deescalates pride while maintaining peace. Godly women don't fight to be right, they fight to stay righteous.

When he avoids responsibility or deflects blame:

Don't chase explanation. State the truth in love: *"I value honesty and accountability. I don't expect perfection, but I do expect ownership."* That tone invites maturity without trying to mother him.

When he asks for your input:

Give it with grace, not dominance. *"Here's what I think...but let's pray about it before we decide. I want God to lead our decision."* That invites collaboration and reminds both of you who's really leading the relationship.

When you feel overlooked:

Don't beg for attention. Bring it to God first. Let Him check your heart before you resort to checking that man's phone. Then, if needed, speak with clarity, not emotion: *"I've noticed some distance. I value communication, so if something's changed, let's be honest about it."*

These moments don't just reveal his character—they refine yours. Every response is an opportunity to practice emotional maturity and spiritual discipline.

Being a Godly, feminine woman doesn't mean you let everything slide. It means you handle everything with composure. You can correct without controlling, confront without condemning, and walk away without bitterness.

And here's what's most attractive to a Godly man: peace that doesn't come from passivity, but from presence. Strength that isn't loud, but consistent. The kind of woman who knows how to bring calm to chaos: not by changing him, but by reflecting Christ.

The beauty of balance is that it holds no matter who's watching. Whether he steps up or falls short, your posture remains the same—rooted, wise, and Spirit-led.

That's what it looks like to lead like a daughter of the King.

When you understand your femininity the way God designed it, you stop performing and start partnering. You stop waiting to be chosen and start walking in your calling.

And that's exactly what we're unpacking next: how to live, lead, and love from your kingdom identity, not just your relationship status.

...

Reflection

Before we move on, pause here. The goal of this chapter isn't to make you "softer" for someone else. It's to help you stand in who God designed you to be. Biblical femininity isn't performance. It's walking in wisdom, grace, and authority that reflect His heart in every space you enter.

1. *Which area do you struggle with more: control or trust? What might it look like to surrender that area to God this week?*

2. *How do you usually respond when a man's behavior disappoints you? What would a Spirit-led response look like instead?*

3. *Which of your strengths have turned into self-protection? How can you let God reshape them into peace and partnership?*

12| A Bride Before the Ring

Before you are a wife to any man, you are already the bride of Christ. That truth sounds poetic, but it's also practical. It changes everything about how you see yourself and how you show up in love. When you understand that you already belong, you stop living like you're waiting to be chosen.

A lot of us were raised to believe marriage is the reward for becoming whole. We fast, pray, and prepare like we're interviewing for a position; trying to prove we're ready for the next season. But what if the real preparation was never about the wedding day? What if it's about the *walk*?

In Scripture, Jesus calls Himself the Bridegroom—the One who pursues, commits to, and covers His Bride, the Church. It's more than a title. It's a picture of covenant love.

In the culture of Jesus' time, weddings didn't happen overnight. They began with a betrothal, which was a binding promise to marry that carried the same weight as marriage itself. From that day forward, the bride and groom belonged to one another, even though they didn't live together yet.

After the betrothal, the groom would give a gift or payment to the bride's family: not to buy her, but to honor her. It was a public declaration that he valued her and was willing to give something costly to prove his commitment. It showed her he was serious about caring for her future.

Then, the groom would leave his bride to prepare a home for her: usually adding living space to his father's house. While he was gone, her job was to stay ready. She never knew the exact day or hour he'd return, so she lived in a constant state of preparation—her lamp filled, her garments clean, her heart expectant.

When the home was ready, the groom would return, often at night, leading a joyful procession through the streets to bring his bride home. Then came the party, a wedding feast that lasted seven days.

That's the picture Jesus gave when He said, *"I go to prepare a place for you...and I will come again and receive you to Myself"* (John 14:2-3 NKJV). He is the Bridegroom who left His Father's house, paid the highest price, and promised to return for His bride.

A bridegroom isn't just a man waiting at the altar. He's the one who prepares, provides, and pursues. That's what Jesus did, and still does, for us.

So, when the Bible calls us the bride of Christ, it means this love story started long before you ever had a "type" or a timeline. You are already spoken for: fully known, fully loved, and already in covenant with a Bridegroom who laid down His life for you.

Isaiah 62:5 says, *"As a bridegroom rejoices over his bride, so will your God rejoice over you"* (Isaiah 62:5 NIV). You were never meant to chase belonging. You were created to live from it.

When you really sit with that, it changes your posture. You don't beg for attention because you recognize the value you carry. You don't chase connection because you carry the weight of covenant. You live *from* love, not *for* it.

This is the part of the journey where faith gets personal. You've healed, you've grown, you've learned how to walk in Godly strength and softness. But now, God is inviting you deeper; to see yourself not just as his daughter, but as His bride.

Because daughters are loved by birthright.
Brides are loved by choice.

And Jesus chose you, not because you're flawless, but because He's faithful. This chapter isn't about earning that love. It's about learning to live from it.

Doing Life With Jesus

Covenant sounds like a big spiritual word, but at its core, it's simply *relationship*. It's not a contract you sign, but a life you share.

Doing life with Jesus means letting Him into the parts of your story you've tried to manage alone. It's not just quiet time in the morning or church on Sunday. It's inviting Him into the group chat, the work meeting, the heartbreak, the plans, and the pause.

Real covenant doesn't clock out when life gets messy. It draws closer.

When you said yes to salvation, you didn't just receive forgiveness. You entered a relationship with the One who promises to walk with you through everything. He doesn't just love you in the highlight reel. He loves you through the ugliness of the process, through the pruning, through the parts of yourself you're still learning to surrender.

Jesus as Bridegroom isn't an image of distance. It's a promise of devotion. He's not waiting for you to get it right. He's asking you to walk with Him while you learn.

Doing life with Jesus looks like talking to Him before you talk to everyone else. It's asking, *"God, what do You think?"* before reacting to what someone said. It's letting Him guide how you respond, what you post, how you love, and how you recover.

It's not performance. It's partnership.

When you live in a way that builds your rhythm around His presence, you begin to see that holiness isn't about perfection. It's about proximity. You stop striving to reach Him. Instead, you keep learning to stay close to Him.

That's what covenant love really is: no rules, but relationship. Not pressure, but presence. Covenant isn't built halfway through the story. It starts from the very beginning. Too many of us invite God in when things start breaking, not realizing He was meant to be the architect, not the fixer. Once you experience that kind of intimacy with Jesus, every other relationship in your life has to rise to that standard.

From Daughter to Bride

When you first come to know God, you meet Him as a Father. He teaches you who you are, how to trust, and what love feels like when it's safe. You learn that you're cared for, covered, and claimed, no questions asked. That's the beauty of being a daughter.

But as you grow, God invites you into a deeper kind of relationship: one built on partnership, not just provision. This is where you move from being a daughter who's dependent to a bride who's devoted. It's the difference between saying, *"God, take care of me,"* and *"God, walk with me as I carry what You've trusted me to do."*

A daughter learns worth.
A bride learns her role in the Kingdom.

But here's the thing. You never stop being a daughter. You don't trade one identity for the other. You learn to live in both. Ephesians 5:25-27 paints the picture clearly: Christ's love sanctifies His bride, cleansing her by the washing of the Word. That's what maturity looks like. You stay the child who runs to her Father for comfort, while becoming the bride who kneels in surrender at His feet. You love Him for His covering and also for His character. You need Him, and you choose Him.

Real covenant looks like dependency that matures into devotion.

Being a bride means learning to love Jesus back, not out of duty, but out of desire. It's choosing closeness when distraction is easier. It's saying yes to His correction because you trust His heart. It's learning to wait, to serve, to forgive, to stay faithful: even when you don't have all the answers.

That's the kind of love that mirrors the heart of Christ. The love that says, *"Even if You don't give me what I want, I'll still give You my whole heart."*

God doesn't just want your obedience. All of creation obeys Him, even demons. He wants your partnership—a daily rhythm of walking with Him, not just running to Him when life falls apart.

This is what spiritual maturity looks like: moving from asking, *"What can You do for me?"* to *"How can I honor You with my life?"*

When you live like that, your faith stops being fragile. You stop living from insecurity and start living from intimacy. You stop trying to prove your worth and start embracing a life of peace.

That's what it means to grow from daughter to bride. It's learning to live as a woman who is forever a Daddy's girl, and yet daily chooses to love Him like His bride.

Do It for the Kingdom, Not the Culture

When you understand who you are to God, it changes how you move in the world. You stop living for validation and start living in victory. You realize that your choices—in love, in work, in how you carry yourself —don't just represent you. They reflect the Kingdom you belong to.

Culture says, *"Do what makes you happy."*
Kingdom says, *"Do what makes you holy."*

Culture says, *"Match their energy."*
Kingdom says, *"Set the standard."*

And the difference is everything.

When you live for culture, you'll always be chasing applause. When you live for the Kingdom, you'll start producing fruit. It shows up in the quiet choices: what you post online, how you handle disappointment, how you talk about people when they're not in the room. It shows up in your relationships, too.

When you're living for the Kingdom, you date with intention, not pressure. You forgive quicker. You listen longer. You walk away sooner when things don't line up. You don't confuse interest with intimacy or chemistry with commitment.

A Kingdom mindset doesn't just change *how* you date, it changes *why*. You're not auditioning for approval; you're discerning for alignment. You're asking, *"Would he fit into my sacred space with Jesus?"* instead of *"Does he make me feel wanted?"*

Culture dates for validation.

Kingdom dates for transformation.

That shift keeps you grounded. You can enjoy the process of getting to know someone without losing yourself in it. You can stay hopeful without being desperate.

A Kingdom woman doesn't chase chemistry, she tests character. She's not afraid to walk away from something that looks good if it costs her peace with God. Because the goal was never just marriage. It's maturity. Philippians 3:14 (KJV) says it plainly: "I press toward the mark for the prize of the high calling of God in Christ Jesus." The real finish line isn't marriage; it's faithfulness.

You're not looking for someone to complete you; you're looking for someone who complements what God is already doing in you. And that mindset doesn't stop at dating. It becomes a lifestyle. Every decision becomes an act of worship. How you show up to work. How you treat people who can't offer you anything in return. How you respond when God says, "Wait."

Culture thrives on speed, noise, and appearance. The Kingdom grows in stillness, obedience, and authenticity. When you live that way, people notice: not because you're trying to impress them, but because you're walking differently. You carry peace in a world that profits off chaos. You carry clarity in a culture that worships confusion.

That's what it means to be a standard-bearer, not to be better than other, but to live so aligned with God that your life quietly invites others to ask, *"What's different about her?"*

Kingdom living isn't loud. It's consistent. It's the steady witness of a woman who knows where her worth comes from and Who she belongs to.

Postured and Prepared

Knowing who you belong to is just the beginning. The real question is, how are you preparing for the One who's coming back for you?

Preparation isn't about fear, striving, or spiritual performance. It's about partnership. Every day becomes a rehearsal for eternity. Every act of obedience, forgiveness, and surrender is part of becoming the woman Christ already sees in you.

The Bible doesn't call us to wait passively, but to *watch* actively: to stay alert, devoted, and ready. Jesus said in Matthew 25 that when the Bridegroom returned, only the women who had oil in their lamps were prepared. The others had lamps too, but no oil left to keep their flame alive. That oil represents intimacy. You can't borrow it, fake it, or rush it. The oil you carry comes from time spent with Him in prayer, in His word, and in surrender.

So how do you prepare for His return while still living your everyday life?

Stay Ready

Every bride prepares differently. Some focus on the ceremony, others the vows. Spiritually, it's both. Readiness starts with your posture: how you approach your day, your purpose, and your relationship with God.

Start your morning by asking, "Lord, what do You want to do through me today?" instead of, "What do I need to get done?" That question changes everything. It keeps your heart soft, your motives pure, and your focus steady. When you walk with God like that, repentance becomes a rhythm: a daily realignment instead of a last-minute rescue.

You start noticing the small things that pull you off course, like comparing your life to others, and you catch them early. Because readiness begins in the heart long before it shows up in your habits.

Walk It Out

Preparation shows up in the small things. It's not glamorous, but it's steady. The way you talk to God, handle people, and manage what's in your hands says more about your readiness than any plan for the future ever could.

Pray honestly, not formally. Talk to God about what you feel, not just what you think you should say. Obey quickly, even when it costs your comfort. Delayed obedience might feel safe, but it's still disobedience. Steward what's in front of you—your money, your work, your friendships—as if Heaven is watching, because it is. Forgive fast. Nothing drains your spirit faster than bitterness disguised as boundaries. Serve quietly. The Bridegroom sees what the crowd doesn't.

Real devotion looks like small, daily yeses that keep your heart in check. The goal isn't to look busy for God, but to stay available to Him. He's not coming back for a hustling bride, but a ready one: a woman who's learned to build while she believes.

Live For Later

Eternity changes everything. When you live with forever in mind, even the ordinary moments start to feel sacred. How you steward your finances, how you treat people, how you show up when you're alone all start pointing to something bigger than you.

Living for later doesn't mean ignoring today. It means seeing today through the lens of tomorrow. You stop chasing quick fixes and start investing in fruit that lasts: peace that can't be shaken, wisdom that doesn't age out, and love that leaves people better than when you found them.

This world will try to convince you that everything urgent is important. It's not. Eternity teaches you to slow down and discern. To ask, *"Will this matter in five years? In fifty? In forever?"* When you think like that, patience becomes easier. Forgiveness feels lighter. Obedience stops feeling like loss and starts looking like legacy.

Heaven isn't just a destination. It's a perspective. Jesus said, *"The kingdom of God is within you."* (Luke 17:21). And when you live for later, you stop striving to build a name and start living to reflect His.

One of the biggest lessons I had to learn is that marriage is a calling: a Kingdom assignment. God isn't just giving you a partner, He's entrusting you with someone else's life.

That's a holy responsibility.

For a long time, I saw marriage as the next level of love: the proof that I had arrived somewhere emotionally or spiritually. But when God began to heal my perspective, I realized marriage isn't a reward for good behavior or a finish line for the faithful. It's stewardship. It's ministry. It's two people carrying the weight of covenant together, with Christ at the center.

But truth be told: not everyone is called to it.
That's not punishment, it's placement. God designs each of us for different Kingdom assignments. Some will be called to build families that reflect His heart. Others will be called to build movements, ministries, and businesses that carry His light in different ways. Some will do both. Both are sacred. Both matter.

If you sense God calling you to marriage, preparation is your responsibility. Not performing to get a partner, but allowing the Holy Spirit to shape your character for covenant. Ask yourself: *Am I becoming more like Jesus every day?*

Here's what the call often looks like in real life:

- A steady, Spirit-led desire for marriage: no pressure, no panic.
- Peace that stays through prayer: no anxiety that rises from comparison.
- Confirmation that comes through Scripture, community, and counsel: not just a prophecy that tickles your ears.

And if the call hasn't come, that's not failure. It's freedom. Freedom to grow. Freedom to serve. Freedom to enjoy the life God has placed in front of you. We are all called to live a fully abundant life.

Being a bride isn't about waiting for a wedding. It's about walking in readiness. Whether or not you ever wear a ring, you're already spoken for. This is why preparation matters. Marriage is only one reflection of a greater calling: to live ready, to walk in holiness, and to become the kind of bride who looks like her Groom. Spiritual, emotional, and practical preparation all begin here.

Spiritual Prep:
Foundation Over Fantasy

I've made my share of wrong choices. I've been single, married, and divorced...and every stage taught me something about myself, about God, and about the kind of love that lasts. I've dated out of loneliness instead of purpose. I've mistaken attention for affection and chemistry for calling. If I could sit with my younger self, I'd tell her this:

Don't chase the version of love that looks good in pictures. Chase the one that does the hard work when no one is watching. I know how easy it is to build your dreams on chemistry, timing, and imagination. I did that. I mistook butterflies for confirmation and loneliness for love. But I learned the hard way that fantasy will always fade. Foundation won't.

Marriage is not a fairytale; it's a mirror.

And not the kind that slims your curves — it's that five-times magnified one that shows every pore, every scar, every place you swore was "healed enough." Covenant doesn't conceal what's broken. It magnifies it. But what seems like cruelty is actually God's mercy. He uses marriage to reveal what comfort singleness let you hide. He exposes what He still intends to restore.

Before you pray for a husband, build your history with God.

A wife after His heart is a woman rooted in Him first. That means learning to hear His voice before following anyone else's, and letting His Word define love before a man ever does. Study covenant: know what God calls love, submission, leadership, and forgiveness. Stay planted in a community that keeps you accountable and helps you grow. Because wholeness isn't something you gain when you're married. It's what you carry into marriage.

If I could go back, here's what I'd whisper to the girl who thought love would save her from herself:

1. Healing isn't optional.

Whatever you hide in singleness will stare back at you in marriage. Your spouse becomes a mirror that reflects the parts of you still under construction. Don't fear the reflection: face it. Let holiness keep highlighting what still needs healing: the father (or mother) wounds, the bitterness, the cycles that keep circling back. Let God treat the wound before someone else touches it. Because what you refuse to surrender now will eventually shape how you love later.

2. Don't pick your scabs.

Healing takes time, and time tests obedience. In singleness, it's easy to stay busy achieving, serving, and living. But busyness isn't an indication of growth. Sometimes God asks you to sit still while He works beneath the surface. Don't go back to the habits, people, or distractions He's trying to deliver you from. That's like peeling off a scab before it's ready: it only reopens what He was trying to close. Sit in the process. Let patience do its work because it's proof that you trust His pace.

3. God's timing is protection, not punishment.

God's timing can feel like delay, like God is holding out on you. But, behind the scenes, it's Him building you up. What feels like waiting is often training. Maturity doesn't grow in comfort, it grows in surrender. We think we know what we need and when we're ready, but His view stretches far beyond our line of sight. He sees the weight of what we're asking for and the strength we'll need to carry it. God will never send you into a promise unprepared or unequipped. So, when He pauses the plan, it's not rejection: it's refinement.

4. Stop performing for promises.

You don't have to audition for God's love or prove your worthiness to be chosen. God's blessings aren't rewards for perfection, they are displays of His affection. He's not looking for the most polished woman. He's shaping the most surrendered one. When you try to perform your way into a promise, you end up exhausted and disconnected from grace. Let Him grow the parts of you that can sustain the very thing you're praying for. His goal isn't to impress you with speed. It's to prepare you with substance.

5. Pray to discern, not to confirm.

I used to ask God to bless what I'd already decided. That's not discernment; that's negotiation. Wisdom prays with open hands, not closed fists. It says, "Lord, show me what's true, even if it unravels what I want." God isn't interested in cosigning our plans. He's committed to protecting our purpose. When you pray for discernment, you invite His vision over your desire. And that's how you recognize the difference between distraction and destiny.

If I could tell that younger version of me anything else, it would be this:

Love will stretch you. Marriage will sanctify you. God will use both to make you whole. Don't fear the mirror: face it with Him. Because when your foundation is truth, even the cracks become places where His light gets in.

Emotional Prep:
From Wounded to Whole

Marriage doesn't heal broken hearts. It exposes them. Emotional maturity doesn't just happen. It's cultivated. And God can't trust us to build with someone else until we've learned how to manage what's going on inside of us. I used to think that spiritual growth alone would prepare me for marriage, but I learned that an unhealed heart will out-talk your prayers and undo your peace.

We've all heard the saying," If you don't deal with what hurt you, you'll end up bleeding on someone who didn't cut you." I've definitely done my share of bleeding.

I used to think I was ready for marriage because I could quote Scripture and pray through problems. But emotional maturity isn't measured by how spiritual you sound. It's revealed by how you handle what hurts. I carried wounds into marriage that I didn't even know were still bleeding. I thought love would heal them. Instead, marriage exposed them.

God used that season to show me that emotional healing isn't a one-time event. It's a lifelong surrender. I had to face the parts of me that shut down when things got hard, the pride that made me defensive, and the fear that made me silent. Healing didn't happen overnight. It came through honesty, therapy, prayer, and community: the slow, steady kind of growth that God measures in years, not weeks.

If I could go back, I'd tell that version of me: "Stop rushing to be ready. Let God rebuild you first." Because when you walk in wholeness, you stop using relationships as medicine. And you stop making people pay for pain they didn't cause.

That's what emotional preparation really is: learning to love from a healed place. Here's what that journey taught me:

1. Learn to self-regulate

Emotions aren't sinful, but they do make poor leaders. I used to let mine decide the tone of my conversation and the pace of every decision. Later I learned that what I called "being real" was often being reactive. Scripture says, *"Be quick to listen, slow to speak, and slow to become angry"* (James 1:19 NIV). That verse became my training ground.

Self-regulation is really Spirit-regulation. It's letting the Holy Spirit interrupt the spiral before your words do damage and also trusting Him to nudge you when silence would cause it. Wisdom isn't found in always holding your tongue or always using it. It's knowing when your words bring life and when your quiet keeps peace.

Maturity looks like pausing long enough to ask, "Is this response led by peace or pride? Is my silence rooted in fear or in faith?" The more we practice that pause, the more we sound like the Bride who's learned her Groom's voice.

2. Practice vulnerability with God and safe people.

I used to think being guarded made me wise. I told myself, *"If I keep my walls high, I won't get hurt again."* But those walls don't just keep people out. They kept my healing out too. Scripture reminds us *"Confess your sins to one another and pray for one another, that you may be healed"* (James 5:16 ESV). Healing flows through honesty.

Vulnerability isn't exposure for sympathy. It's surrender that brings restoration. God doesn't ask us to open up because He needs the details. He asks because He knows we heal in truth, not denial. And He often uses safe community as His hands and heart to reach the places we hide.

Being the Bride of Christ means learning to trust His covering, to believe you're safe enough to be seen. When we let His love name us, shame loses its power. Openness becomes strength, not weakness.

3. Understand your triggers before someone else trips them.

I used to get defensive and think everybody else was the problem. Any time something brushed against an old wound, I took it as a sign that person wasn't "safe." What I didn't realize was that my triggers were teachers, not enemies. They were revealing where healing still had work to do. Scripture says, *"Search me, O God, and know my heart...see if there is any offensive way in me, and lead me in the way everlasting"* (Psalm 139:23-24 NIV).

Let God search you before you expect someone else to understand you. When we ignore our triggers, they end up running our relationships. But when we invite the Holy Spirit to shine light on them, He turns them from landmines into lessons.

Self-awareness is a form of stewardship. It's saying, "Lord, help me recognize what's mine to heal so I don't project it onto someone You've sent to love me." That's how the Bride becomes emotionally safe—not just waiting to be protected but becoming a place of peace herself.

4. Replace fear-based independence with healthy partnership.

For a long time, I mistook independence for strength. I told myself I didn't need anyone because needing people had always led to disappointment. I called it protecting my peace, but really, I was protecting my pain. God didn't design us to do life alone. Even Jesus chose twelve. Scripture says, *"Two are better than one...if either of them falls down, one can help the other up"* (Ecclesiastes 4:9-10 NIV).

Healthy partnership doesn't mean losing yourself. It means letting love teach you balance. You can be whole and still need help. You can be wise and still ask for counsel. Maturity is knowing how to receive support without shrinking and how to give it without control.

When the Bride learns this, she stops confusing walls with wisdom. She learns that strength isn't in isolation. It's in unity that mirrors the heart of God.

5. Guard your heart, but don't harden it.

After my marriage ended, I remember asking myself, *"How did I get here?"* Single again at thirty-eight. I wasn't just upset about being alone while knocking on forty's door. I was wrestling with bitterness, anger, and the quiet humiliation of feeling like I'd failed. The thought of marriage again felt pointless. I couldn't imagine trying to build something I no longer trusted myself to sustain.

So, I built higher walls around my heart, thinking they would keep me safe. I told myself I was "guarding my heart," but I was really just locking it away. Scripture says, *"Above all else, guard your heart, for everything you do flows from it"* (Proverbs 4:23 NIV). Guarding doesn't mean closing the gate, it means knowing what and who to let through. It also means knowing what to release: the resentment, the shame, and fear that choke out new growth.

A hardened heart keeps out pain, but it also keeps out love. God's kind of guarding looks like walking with wisdom. He teaches us to set boundaries without bitterness and to stay soft without being naïve.

The Bride of Christ doesn't love behind walls. She lives under covering. Her safety isn't in control. It's in the confidence that her Groom protects what belongs to Him. When you trust that, you can love freely, forgive quickly, and stay tender even when life gives you every reason to shut down.

Practical Prep:
Faithful with the "Little"

God doesn't skip steps, and He never wastes seasons. But sometimes we treat stewardship like it's optional, as if managing what's already in our hands is less important that praying for what's next. But faithfulness isn't busy work. It's worship. Every time you show up, plan well, keep your word, or clean up your space, you're telling God, *"You can trust me with more."*

Luke 16:10 says, *"Whoever can be trusted with very little can also be trusted with much"* (Luke 16:10 NIV). In other words, the "little" seasons are not pointless. They're preparation. God watches how we manage what we already have before He multiplies it. Society tells us to always want more, but Heaven asks, *"What are you doing with what I already gave you?"*

Faithfulness doesn't always stand out, but it stands firm. The world celebrates what looks impressive, but God honors what's consistent. Managing your life well may not get applause, but it builds credibility. And a Godly man will notice that. A woman who handles her responsibilities with grace, order, and wisdom doesn't need to chase love. The right one will recognize the fruit of her faithfulness.

Here's what that looks like in practice:

1. Steward your money like it's ministry.

Budget, pay off debt, and build savings: not for status, but to show God you value what He's placed in your hands. How you handle money is a mirror of how you handle responsibility. Proverbs 21:20 (NLT) says, *"The wise have wealth and luxury, but fools spend whatever they get."* In other words, wisdom plans ahead, and foolishness spends without thought.

Start where you are. Look at your bank statement and ask, *"Does this reflect discipline or distraction?"* If funds are tight, simplify your spending so you can stay consistent. Cook more at home, cancel subscriptions you don't use or need, and find joy in small progress—even if it's saving five dollars at a time. Make it a goal to live within your means. God doesn't need perfection. He honors progress. Every wise decision is a seed that grows trust with Him. And learning to trust Him with the little that you have is how God prepares you to handle much when it comes.

And if you're in a season of abundance, stewardship still matters. Having more doesn't mean removing responsibility. It multiplies it. Build a plan that honors God and protects your future. Give faithfully. Invest wisely. Save strategically. Pray before major purchases. Ask God, *"Is this a need, a desire, or a distraction?"* Enjoy what He's given you, but keep your spending anchored in gratitude, not impulse. Wealth is safest in the hands of those who remember where it came from. When He's part of the process, even your spending becomes a form of surrender.

And remember, generosity is one of the purest ways to keep wealth from owning you. Give privately, give joyfully, and give often: not to prove your goodness, but to reflect His. Use your abundance to multiply impact, not just income. Support a ministry. Fund a mission trip. Pay a bill for someone quietly. The goal isn't to give until it hurts. It's to give until it humbles.

Stewardship in scarcity builds trust. Stewardship in abundance builds humility. Both please God. Whether you're managing hundreds or hundreds of thousands, the call is the same: to treat every dollar as a tool for worship, not a measure of worth. Faithfulness isn't about the amount in your hands. It's about the posture of your heart.

2. Build structure that serves you, not strains you.

Discipline is one of the purest forms of devotion. The Proverbs 31 woman wasn't an ideal Christian woman because she did everything. It was because she was purposeful and did what mattered. Her strength came from order, not overworking.

For a single woman walking with God, balance is more about rhythm than routine. It's learning to make time for what keeps your spirit fed, your soul full, and your life steady.

Make prayer a part of your day the same way you plan to eat breakfast, lunch, and dinner: necessary for strength, not optional for convenience. Set aside moments to read and study your Word, not just when life feels heavy but when it feels good too. You build intimacy with God through consistency, not crisis.

Structure also means making room for joy. Schedule a solo date just to enjoy your own company. Take yourself to brunch, walk through a farmer's market, or watch a movie you've been wanting to see. These moments remind you that you are worthy of intentional care, not just survival.

And don't overlook rest. Rest is holy. Build it into your week like it's an appointment with God, because it is. When you rest, you acknowledge that your worth isn't found in what you produce.

Discipline shows up in details: cleaning your space so your mind can breathe, putting your phone on do not disturb so your spirit can stay clear, creating goals that stretch your faith but protect your peace. A well-balanced life doesn't mean you have every box checked. It means you've learned how to protect the life God has trusted you with.

A woman of wisdom knows her pace and keeps it sacred. She doesn't run herself empty chasing everything. She stays faithful in the few things that fill her. That's what makes her steady, and ready, for whatever God builds next.

3. Communicate with grace before crisis.

Communication is where maturity either shows up or breaks down. I used to think good communication meant saying everything I felt in the moment. But I learned that sometimes silence is wisdom, and other times, silence is avoidance. Grace knows the difference.

Marriage won't magically make you a better communicator. It will magnify whatever habits you already have. So, practice now. Let God teach you how to speak without hostility and listen without defense. The goal isn't to win arguments. It's to win understanding.

Scripture says, *"Let no corrupting talk come out of your mouths, but only what is helpful for building others up"* (Ephesians 4:29 ESV). That doesn't mean you can't express hard things. It means you express them from a heart that wants healing, not victory. There's a way to be honest without being harsh; to tell the truth in love instead of using truth as a weapon.

And sometimes grace looks like restraint: praying before responding, stepping away before speaking. But grace also has a backbone. There are moments when you'll need to speak up for yourself, to set boundaries, or to address conflict instead of burying it. Healthy communication doesn't mean avoiding tension. It means handling it with spiritual maturity.

Start with the people around you. When a friend disappoints you, talk through it instead of talking around it. When your boss frustrates you, choose clarity over gossip. When family conversations get heated, stay rooted in peace. Every time you choose composure over chaos, you're rehearsing covenant.

Communication is not just about words. It's also about witness. How you talk to others reveals how much time you've spent with God. The woman who learns to speak with grace before the crisis doesn't just build peace in her relationships. She carries peace into every room she enters.

4. Let integrity be your atmosphere.

Integrity is not just what you believe, but how you behave. It's who you are when no one is clapping and who you stay when no one is checking. The goal isn't to impress people. It's to honor God with a life that tells the truth, even when you're not speaking.

For me, integrity used to feel like a big idea; something reserved for leaders or pastors. But over time I realized it's built in the smallest choices. It's showing up to work on time when you'd rather sleep. It's closing your laptop when you've done enough instead of "stealing time". It's keeping a promise to yourself—to eat better, to pray longer, to forgive quicker—even when no one else would notice if you didn't.

Proverbs 10:9 (NIV) says, *"Whoever walks in integrity walks securely."* When your public life and your private life match, you can breathe easy. There's a peace in knowing you don't have to juggle two versions of yourself.

Integrity is also how you handle temptation, not just sexual temptation, but being tempted to compromise character for comfort. It's choosing conviction when cutting corners would be easier. It's walking away from conversations that feed gossip, scrolling past what stirs comparison, and repenting quickly when you miss the mark.

A woman who walks in integrity doesn't have to chase credibility. Her consistency will build it. She becomes trustworthy because she's true. And that kind of security can't be faked or fabricated. It's formed in secret with God.

Live like someone who knows He's watching: not in fear, but in reverence. Let your integrity speak louder than your image. Because when your atmosphere is honest, your influence will always carry Heaven's weight.

When the "Little" Becomes Much

Faithfulness with the "little" is what shapes a woman God can trust with more. Whether that "little" looks like a small paycheck, a studio apartment, a new job, or simply the quiet season of being unseen. This is where foundations are built. The habits you form now will hold the weight of what you're praying for.

Every budget, boundary, and act of obedience is worship. Every time you show up, even when no one's watching, you're proving to Heaven that you can carry the next level of responsibility with grace. These disciplines don't just make life easier; they make your spirit stronger.

God isn't just watching what you do; He's watching *how* you do it. He blesses order, He breathes on diligence, and He multiplies what's managed well. Faithfulness is not about impressing Him. It's about imitating Him.

Whatever season you're in, manage it with intention. Steward your time, your gifts, your words, and your resources like they belong to Someone holy, because they do. The "little" you're holding now is training for the "much" that's coming.

Relational Prep:
Community Before Covenant

Healthy love grows in healthy soil. Before there was a wedding there was a garden. Adam walked with God before Eve ever entered the picture, and that walk shaped how he loved her. The same is true for us. Relationship prep doesn't start with dating. It starts with how you treat the people God's already placed in your life.

A lot of women pray for partnership but isolate themselves in the meantime. We convince ourselves that "no one understands" or "it's just me and God," but isolation often hides immaturity. God uses community to grow what solitude can't. You'll never learn patience, empathy, or forgiveness in theory…only in relationship.

Love doesn't start at the altar. It starts in the soil. Before you ever walk in covenant with someone else, God will teach you how to love well in community. This is where you practice the posture of partnership: how to listen, serve, forgive, and stay faithful when it's inconvenient. You can't skip the classroom of connection and expect to graduate into covenant. The same patience, humility, and empathy that make a marriage thrive are formed in friendship, in service, and in everyday moments of choosing people over pride.

So, before you pray for a ring, look at your roots. Ask yourself, *"Am I learning to love well right where I am?"* That's where relational preparation begins. Here's what it looks like:

1. Your squad matters: find friends who cover and challenge you.

Proverbs 27:17 (NIV) says, *"As iron sharpens iron, so one person sharpens another."* The people closest to you shape how you think, pray, and grow. Accountability is about covering, not control. You need friends who love you enough to tell you the truth, even when it's uncomfortable, and who push you to stay in alignment with God, not your emotions.

For two years, I stepped away from church. I told myself I needed a break, but what I really needed was healing and more bible study. Somewhere along the way, I lost hope that genuine community even existed. I was tired of surface-level conversations, and disappointed by people who didn't show up the way I expected. But self-inflicted isolation doesn't protect you. It slowly drains you.

When I finally had the courage to return, God surrounded me with a church family and a group of women who reminded me why community matters. And my small group leader shared a verse from Hebrews 10:24-25 that changed everything for me. It was a reminder that we're called to encourage one another, to keep each other stirred up in faith, and not to walk this journey alone. The truth hit me deep: I wasn't designed to do life solo. I was designed to grow sharper *with* others.

The right squad will check your blind spots and protect your progress. They'll pray with you when you're weak and celebrate you when you win. But they'll also correct you when you're slipping. That's what sharpening looks like.

And it goes both ways. Be the kind of friend who guards things said in confidence, who speaks life instead of gossip, who cheers for other women like their victories don't threaten your own. Real accountability isn't one-sided. It's mutual refinement. The way you show up in friendship is often how you'll show up in partnership.

2. You learn love by serving.

If you want to understand covenant, start with compassion. Love doesn't grow in comfort; it grows in service. Before God trusts you to build a home with someone, He'll often test how well you build with others. Serving trains your heart for partnership and it teaches you to put love in action instead of leaving it in theory.

When I think about the seasons I grew the most, they were the ones where I was pouring out, not being poured into. Helping at church. Babysitting for a single mom. And, especially taking care of my mother when she was sick. Showing up for someone, even when it's inconvenient, stretches your heart and strips your pride. It teaches you to see needs and meet them with grace.

Jesus modeled this perfectly when He washed His disciples' feet (See John 13:1-17). The King of Kings knelt low and called it love. That moment was more than humility: it was leadership. He showed us that greatness in the kingdom isn't measured by how many people serve you, but by how many people you're willing to serve.

Serving also shifts your perspective. It quiets entitlement. It reminds you that your gifts aren't just for your own success but for someone else's breakthrough. When you serve with joy—whether that's greeting at the church door, mentoring a teen, helping a coworker who's struggling, or just listening to a friend—you begin to reflect God's heart in action.

And here's the beautiful part. What you learn in service translates to every relationship. The same humility that helps you serve a team will help you love your husband. The same patience it takes to deal with difficult people will help you handle conflict with grace. The same faithfulness you practice in community becomes the endurance that holds covenant together.

Wherever you are, serve well. Don't wait for title, a platform, or a partner to start living with purpose. You learn by serving and the woman who learns to love like that is already on her way to preparing for marriage.

3. Watch without wanting

Observation is one of the most underrated ways to prepare for marriage. God gives us examples not to stir envy but to offer insight. There's wisdom all around you if you're willing to watch with humility.

When I started paying attention to Godly marriages, I realized how much you can learn just by listening and observing. I stopped looking for picture-perfect couples and started watching how they handled pressure, forgiveness, and seasons of change. The couples that inspired me the most weren't the ones who looked happiest on social media. They were the ones who prayed through hardship, laughed through ordinary days, and chose grace over pride when conflict came.

If you have access to a couple whose relationship you respect, ask thoughtful questions. "What's one thing you wish you had learned before marriage?" "How do you stay emotionally connected when life gets busy?" Then listen: not to copy their story, but to catch their principles. God will often let you learn through someone else's experiences so you don't have to repeat their lessons.

But guard your heart while you observe. It's easy to shift from inspiration to comparison if you forget that everyone's timeline is different. Comparison will make you question God's faithfulness. Wisdom will remind you that He cares about your story, too. Be encouraged by what you see, not pressured by it.

Every healthy marriage you witness is a preview of what's possible when two people choose covenant daily. Let those examples build your faith, not your frustration. Watch without wanting. Learn without longing. And trust the same God who's blessing them also knows exactly how to prepare you.

4. Be who you're asking for

At some point in my singleness, I realized I was praying for a type of man, when I hadn't yet become the type of woman to match. I wanted consistency while being unpredictable. I wanted leadership while resisting correction. I wanted godliness while still healing from habits that pulled me away from God. God didn't withhold love from me. He invited me to mature into the kind of love I was asking for.

It's easy to evaluate someone else's readiness. It's harder to look in the mirror and ask, *Am I ready for what I've been praying for?* Discernment isn't just about reading someone else's fruit; it's about tending to your own. Are you emotionally stable enough to communicate without manipulation? Spiritually grounded enough to be led without losing your voice? Financially wise enough to partner without depending?

Before you look for alignment with someone else, check your alignment with God. If He's still working on your patience, forgiveness, or self-control, that's not to punish you. It's God refining what love will one day rely on. He's shaping the kind of heart that can sustain covenant, not just enter it.

And if you do meet someone, hold yourself accountable to the same standards you desire in him. Don't let fear talk you out of what you've been praying for. Sometimes we're so used to spotting red flags that we miss the green ones. When a man shows up with consistency, humility, and Godly character, receive it without suspicion (unless the Holy Spirit tells you differently). Caution protects you, but fear can paralyze you. Let wisdom be your guide, not doubt.

At the same time, stay honest with yourself. Don't ignore red flags because you're afraid to start over, and don't project perfection onto someone just because you're tired of waiting. Wisdom lives in the tension between caution and openness, trusting God enough to love with both eyes open.

At this point, you've done the inner work. You've healed, built discipline, learned to love in community, and practiced discernment in dating. But preparation is only part of the story. God doesn't call us to stay in readiness forever. He calls us to walk in relationship with Him now. The real shift happens when you stop seeing this season as waiting for something to start and begin realizing it already has.

The Shift:
From Waiting to Walking

You've already seen how easily waiting can become a habit. Back in *The Church Said Wait*, we talked about how it can feel like life is on pause until the next thing: the next season, the next door, the next prayer answered. But the truth is, purpose isn't waiting somewhere in the distance. It's already moving with you.

The wait was never wasted. It trained your discernment, strengthened your faith, and shaped your character. You've done the heart work. You've grown roots in places that once felt barren. And now God is saying, *walk*.

Walking doesn't mean rushing ahead. It means showing up with what you've learned. It means living with intention instead of hesitation. You're not preparing for life anymore. You're in it.

This is where the mindset shifts from hoping something happens *to you*, to realizing God is already doing something *through you*. The goal was never to arrive at marriage. It was to arrive at maturity. And now, wherever you go, you walk as someone who's ready: for purpose, for promise, for whatever God writes next.

Walk Authentically

Now that you've learned who you are as a daughter and bride, it's time to *walk* like her. God didn't spend all this time healing, refining, and restoring you just for you to shrink back into a version of yourself that's easy to manage.

He didn't make you unique so you could spend your life blending in.

Authenticity is alignment. It's when your inner life and outer expression finally agree. Too many women confuse holiness with hiding, thinking quiet equals humble or small equals safe. But God isn't glorified by our pretending. He's glorified through the full expression of who He created us to be.

If you're creative, create. If you're funny, laugh loudly. If you're adventurous, explore. Whatever makes you come alive, do it without apology, because God placed that spark in you on purpose. Jesus was fully God and fully man; He felt deeply, celebrated freely, and still carried divine authority. You were made to live that same balance: fully spiritual, fully human, fully alive.

For the woman believing for marriage, this matters more than you realize. Sometimes the reason a Godly man can't recognize you is because you're not walking in the version of yourself God designed. A man submitted to God will recognize your fruit—peace, joy, purpose—but not if you're hiding behind fear, performance, or false humility. God can't bless the mask.

And if marriage isn't your path, this still applies. Living authentically is worship. It tells God, *"I'm grateful for the life You gave me, and I'll live it fully."* Showing up as your true self is one of the purest ways to honor your Creator.

Walk boldly. Smile freely. Lead fearlessly. Be fully you, the woman God had in mind when He called you His own. Because that woman? She's already living in purpose.

From Frustration to Freedom

If this journey has taught you anything, I hope it's this: freedom doesn't always come when life changes. Sometimes it comes when *you* do. Frustration used to feel like proof that God forgot you, but now you know better. It was the tension that grew your trust.

You've learned to stop fighting the timeline and start flowing with the assignment. You've seen how wholeness doesn't guarantee marriage, but it does guarantee peace. The kind that doesn't crumble when life looks different than you expected.

For the woman still believing for marriage, hold that desire with open hands. You don't have to apologize for wanting love. Just remember—marriage is a chapter, not the conclusion. Walk with God (not behind Him or ahead of Him), and you'll never have to chase what He's already aligned for You. When it's time, it'll meet you on your path of purpose, and find you while you're minding your Father's business.

And for the woman who is content, unsure, or no longer desires marriage: your story is no less complete. You are still the bride. Still chosen. Still seen. Freedom for you means living fully in what *is*, not being haunted by what *isn't*. When you show up for your own life with joy and gratitude, you prove that fulfillment was never about a ring. It was about reflection. You reflect His love simply by existing in it.

You started this book frustrated—tired of mixed messages, the waiting games, the pressure to prove yourself worthy of love. But now, you know freedom. The kind that breathes instead of strives. The kind that builds instead of begs.

So keep walking, Sis.
Free.
Full.
Found.

Because although you may not have everything you've prayed for, you've learned to become the woman who trusts the One who hears you, knows you, and loves you.

Build now.
Heal now.
Serve now.
Love Jesus with your whole heart *now*.

You don't have to wait for a ring to start living like you're chosen. You already are. And not just in theory, but in truth. Long before you ever prayed for love, God called you His own. He loved you so much that He sacrificed His life and gave everything up to win your heart. There's no greater love than this! And no man on earth could ever love you this deeply. So, walk in that unconditional love. Walk in confidence. Walk in peace, knowing the same God who calls you His daughter also calls you His bride.

And be proud of yourself. You've done the hard things. You've confronted your idols, faced your fears, and traded fantasy for real foundation. You've learned how to prepare: not waiting, but walking. Not striving but surrendering.

Now, you're ready. Ready to build, to lead, to laugh again. Ready to love fully, not just romantically. Because when you walk in purpose, peace becomes the proof that you're exactly where you belong.

However your story unfolds—with marriage, with ministry, with quiet obedience—you'll know you lived as a bride who was ready. A woman who found her freedom in the Father, at peace in His presence, and confident in who He created her to be.

Go live the rest of your story and be present for *every* chapter He writes.

...

Before you turn the page or close this book, pause for a moment. Take a deep breath and let your heart settle. You've walked through truth, healing, and clarity. But most importantly, you've walked closer to the One who calls you His own.

A Bride's Prayer

*Father, thank You for rewriting
my story with grace.
I release every timeline, fear, and fantasy
that once tried to define me.
Fill me with Your wisdom and Your Word,
and help me live as a bride who is ready.
Faithful, focused, and full of peace.
Let my life reflect Your heart in every
space I step into.*
Amen.

Notes and References

Bible Translation

Scripture quotations are from the New International Version (NIV), unless otherwise noted. Used by permission.

Hebrew Word Studies

- *Matsa* (מָצָא) — The Hebrew word translated as "find" in Proverbs 18:22 means "to discover, to attain, to acquire, to encounter" (Strong's H4672). Source: *Strong's Exhaustive Concordance of the Bible*, by James Strong (1890), accessed via Blue Letter Bible, https://www.blueletterbible.org.

- *Qavah* (קָוָה) — The Hebrew word translated as "wait" in Psalm 27:14 means "to actively look for, to hope with expectation, to entwine your heart with God's while you anticipate what He is doing" (Strong's H6960). Source: *Strong's Exhaustive Concordance of the Bible*, by James Strong (1890), accessed via Blue Letter Bible, https://www.blueletterbible.org.

Additional References

Brown, F., Driver, S. R., & Briggs, C. A. (1906). *The Brown-Driver-Briggs Hebrew and English Lexicon*. Clarendon Press. Retrieved from https://www.blueletterbible.org.
Strong, J. (1890). *The Exhaustive Concordance of the Bible*. Abingdon Press. Retrieved from https://www.blueletterbible.org.

About the Author

Cynthia Hickerson is a writer, speaker, and entrepreneur who helps women grow closer to God and rediscover purpose in every season. Blending biblical truth with lived experience, her words invite readers to heal, think deeply, and live faithfully. She is the author of *Broken-Hearted: 13 Practical Lessons I Learned About Loving God with a Broken Heart* (2020) and *Sis, Break Up With Boaz*, written for single Christian women who are ready to release frustration and embrace freedom in Christ. When she's not writing, Cynthia teaches women how to build wealth through real estate and live with peace, purpose, and joy.

For Groups & Study

This book was written to be read slowly—talked through, prayed through, and lived out. Whether you're studying with friends, a small group, or your women's ministry, take your time. God speaks in layers, and every chapter invites reflection.

If you'd like a simple 8-week rhythm, try this:

Week 1: Chapters 1–2
Week 2: Chapters 3–4
Week 3: Chapter 5
Week 4: Chapter 6
Week 5: Chapter 7
Week 6: Chapter 8
Week 7: Chapters 9-10
Week 8: Chapters 11-12

Each week, read the assigned chapters, then use the Reflection questions to spark honest conversation. Pray together. Listen to one another. Let the Holy Spirit guide what comes up.

If This Book Resonated With You

Thank you for walking this journey with me. *Sis, Break Up With Boaz* was never just about marriage: it's about coming home to God and remembering who you are in Him. If something in these pages stirred your heart, don't keep it to yourself.

Here are a few ways to stay connected and keep growing:

1. **Share your story.**

   Tell me what chapter spoke to you most. I love hearing how God is working in your life. You can connect with me on TikTok and Instagram **@CynthiaSpeaksFaith** and visit my website at www.cynthiaspeaksfaith.com

2. **Leave a review.**

   Your words help other women find this message and remind them they're not alone. Honest reviews mean more than you know.

3. **Invite a friend.**

   Start a small group, host a book chat, or share this book with another woman who's still waiting, wondering, or healing. Freedom multiplies when we walk together.

And above all, remember this:
God was never holding marriage back from you.
He's been holding *you* close the whole time.

www.ingramcontent.com/pod-product-compliance
Lightning Source LLC
Chambersburg PA
CBHW071743120626
46550CB00002B/647